M48 PATTON
VS
CENTURION
Indo-Pakistani War 1965

DAVID R. HIGGINS

First published in Great Britain in 2016 by Osprey Publishing,
PO Box 883, Oxford, OX1 9PL, UK
PO Box 3985, New York, NY 10185-3985, USA
E-mail: info@ospreypublishing.com

Osprey Publishing, part of Bloomsbury Publishing Plc

A CIP catalogue record for this book is available from the British Library

Print ISBN: 978 1 4728 1092 2
PDF ebook ISBN: 978 1 4728 1093 9
ePub ebook ISBN: 978 1 4728 1094 6

Index by Rob Munro
Typeset in ITC Conduit and Adobe Garamond
Maps by bounford.com
Originated by PDQ Media, Bungay, UK
Printed in China through World Print Ltd.

16 17 18 19 20   10 9 8 7 6 5 4 3 2 1

Osprey Publishing supports the Woodland Trust, the UK's leading woodland
conservation charity. Between 2014 and 2018 our donations are being spent
on their Centenary Woods project in the UK.

www.ospreypublishing.com

Acknowledgements

I would like to thank the following individuals for their kind support, without
which this book, and my other military history endeavours, might not have
been possible. Joseph Miranda, editor-in-chief, *Strategy & Tactics* magazine;
Colonel (ret.) Jerry D. Morelock, PhD, editor-in-chief, *Armchair General*
magazine; Major Karun Khanna (Retd); Jagan Pillarisetti; Henrik Teller;
Abhinay Rathore; Umar Bajwa; Imtiaz Ahmed Bajwa; M.P. Robinson; Simon
Dunstan; and my editor, Nick Reynolds. Any errors or omissions in this work
are certainly unintended, and I alone bear responsibility for them.

Editor's note

Metric measurements are used throughout the book. For ease of comparison
please refer to the following conversion table:

1km = 0.62 miles
1m = 1.09yd / 3.28ft
1cm = 0.39in
1mm = 0.04in
1kg = 2.20lb / 35.27oz
1 tonne = 0.98 long (UK) tons / 1.10 short (US) tons
1 litre = 0.22 UK gallons / 0.26 US gallons
1kW = 1.34hp (international)

Glossary

APCBC/HE-T: Armour-Piercing Capped Ballistic Cap/High Explosive – Tracer
APDS: Armour-Piercing Discarding Sabot
APHE-T: Armour-Piercing High Explosive – Tracer
HE: High Explosive
HEAT: High Explosive Anti-Tank
HVAP: High Velocity Armour-Piercing

Title page photograph: Following the Indian victory during the Asal Uttar
fighting south-east of Lahore, some 60 of the 97 captured Pakistani M47 and
M48 Pattons, M24 Chaffees and M4 Shermans were temporarily assembled in
Bhikhiwind. This image of what became known as 'Patton-Nagar' ('Patton
City'), along with numerous other images, dramatically illustrated Pakistan's
defeat – much to India's political benefit. (Brigadier Hari Singh Deora AVSM,
18th Cavalry)

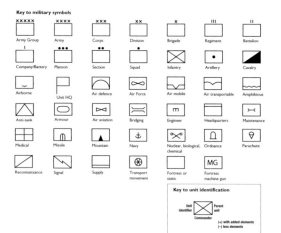

CONTENTS

INTRODUCTION

A disabled Pakistani M48 Patton tank from 6th Armoured Division in the Sialkot sector. Oddly, considering the dry, dusty environment of the Bari Doab – an irrigated region between the Beas and Ravi rivers – the gun shield lacks a canvas cover. During the transition to production status upwards of 6,000 drawings and 2,000 component blueprints for the M48 were created, with some 8,500 parts comprising the vehicle. Improvements over the M47 included a more streamlined hull, an improved suspension, and a T-shaped muzzle brake rather than the M47's cylindrical variety. The change to the muzzle brake meant that rapidly escaping gases on firing were better vented to the sides, and thus less likely to disrupt the immediate ground, which lessened the risk of exposing the firing location. Note the lack of vehicle markings. (Keystone/Getty Images)

At 0330hrs on 1 September 1965, Pakistan Army artillery commenced a three-hour bombardment of Indian Army positions in the disputed territory of Jammu and Kashmir. Pakistani ground forces, tasked with capturing the strategically vital Akhnur Bridge over the Chenab River, launched their attack at 0500hrs; against the key Chumb area along the right, this involved a three-pronged assault, each with a vanguard unit equipped with the formidable US-provided M48 Patton tank, representing the cutting edge of the Pakistan Armoured Corps.

As the northern Pakistani prong swung out of Pir Maungawali for the mountain crossing near Mandiala, the central thrust pushed straight for Chumb. A single squadron of 20th Lancers equipped with AMX-13 light tanks comprised the only Indian armour in the area; these French-built armoured fighting vehicles possessed relatively effective firepower, but lacked sufficient armour protection to survive a lengthy struggle with their heavier Pakistani adversaries. It would be nearly a week before India's Centurion Mk 7 tanks entered the fray, but their contribution would prove crucial to the outcome of the war, as senior Indian commanders embarked on their plans to take the conflict into Pakistani territory.

Even though Indian war games in 1955–56 had focused on defending against such an assault along the Chumb–Jourian–Akhnur axis, in 1965 senior Indian commanders had generally dismissed such an eventuality, choosing to believe that Pakistan would avoid directly invading India proper; instead, they anticipated an attack further north in the Naushahra–Rajauri–Jhangar sector. Having formulated a plan (Operation *Riddle*) following recent events in the Rann of Kutch, Indian strategy was to hold in Kashmir, where Pakistani forces' logistical lines were shorter, potentially strike for Karachi or Rawalpindi, and draw Pakistani forces from the primary fight in the present battle zone in Punjab.

After decades of confrontation and months of escalation, India and Pakistan were now engaged in open warfare, and the world watched closely. Such a conflict offered a rare arena in which US- and British-supplied military hardware, albeit largely of World War II vintage, would fight against each other. While India was saddled with outdated M3A3 Stuart and M4 Sherman tanks, its fleet of post-1945 Centurion tanks with 20-pdr main guns offered a degree of parity against a contemporary armoured adversary. Similarly encumbered with the outdated M36 Jackson tank destroyer, M24 Chaffee light tank and M4 Sherman medium tank, all of which were past their battlefield prime, Pakistan also deployed newer, more sophisticated American armour in the shape of the M47 and especially M48 Patton designs which offered the potential to dominate the ground war.

A Centurion Mk 7, with its side skirts removed. Up to three spare track-links could be held on the glacis behind the port headlight. The vehicle appears to be missing a 10.6×5.2m camouflage net commonly stowed atop both locked turret bins, behind which external methyl bromide fire extinguishers were fixed. A water container, No. 1 cable reel assembly and three spare track-lengths occupied the turret rear. Small mirrors – to assist the driver when moving in reverse – on both forward track guards are also absent. The gun shield's canvas cover minimized dust and debris from entering the turret. (M.P. Robinson via Simon Dunstan)

CHRONOLOGY

1943

July — Britain's War Office authorizes development of the A41 Heavy Cruiser Tank.

1944

March — Equipped with M3 Stuart light tanks, No. 1 Troop, A Squadron, 7th Light Cavalry is the first Indian Army armoured unit to see combat, against the Japanese in Burma.

May — Associated Equipment Company Ltd produces a mild-steel A41 mock-up.

1945

25 February — The M26 Pershing, the United States' first heavy tank, makes its combat debut against German forces near the Roer River.

April — Royal Ordnance Factory Woolwich unveils the first A41 prototype.

November — The US War Department Equipment Board outlines a five-year modernization programme for the US Army.

1947

15 August — The Dominion of India and the Dominion of Pakistan come into being.

22 October — The First Indo-Pakistani War begins as Pakistan-backed local forces move into the independent princely state of Jammu and Kashmir; on 26 October the ruler of Jammu and Kashmir signs the Instrument of Accession to the Dominion of India.

1949

1 January — The First Indo-Pakistani War ends, with roughly 40 per cent of Jammu and Kashmir in Pakistani hands and the remainder under Indian control.

27 July — The Karachi Agreement establishes a border along Jammu and Kashmir.

1950

26 January — The Dominion of India becomes the Republic of India, with Dr Rajendra Prasad its first President (until May 1962).

28 June — Three days after North Korean forces cross the 38th Parallel, starting the Korean War, the Army Organization Act makes armour a permanent branch of the US Army; the M26 Pershing heavy tank, having been reclassified as the M46 Patton medium tank, sees widespread action in Korea.

Indian Centurion tanks give a tow to captured Patton tanks from Pakistan's 1st Armoured Division in the Chawinda sector. (bharat-rakshak.com)

1951

27 February	Design of the M48 Patton begins.
22–25 April	Centurion Mk III tanks operated by Britain's 8th King's Royal Irish Hussars see combat at the battle of the Imjin River in Korea.
June	M47 production commences at the Detroit Arsenal Tank Plant.

1952

29 January	First T48 pilot chassis begins a two-week shakedown at Chrysler's Chelsea proving grounds.
1 July	The M48 is officially designated the 'Patton'.

1953

January	Production of the Centurion Mk 7 commences.
2 April	M48 production commences.
27 July	The Korean War ends.

1955

8 September	The M47 Patton is declared 'limited standard' by the United States, having never seen combat with US forces.

1956

23 March	The Dominion of Pakistan becomes the Islamic Republic of Pakistan.

1958

October	A *coup d'état* in Pakistan sees Lieutenant-General Muhammad Ayub Khan, Army Commander-in-Chief and Minister of Defence, take power and combine the offices of president and prime minister.

1962

20 October	The Sino-Indian War begins as Chinese forces move across the disputed Himalayan border between India and China, overwhelming outnumbered Indian forces in two attacks 1,000km apart.
19 November	China declares a unilateral ceasefire;

Aksai Chin, considered by India to be part of Jammu and Kashmir, is now under Chinese control. In 1963 the north-eastern part of Pakistan-controlled Jammu and Kashmir also passes into Chinese hands, although India does not recognize this outcome.

1965

August	Pakistan launches Operation *Gibraltar*, in which paramilitary personnel infiltrate Indian-administered Jammu and Kashmir.
1 September	Operation *Gland Slam*: at 0330hrs, a Pakistani bombardment of Indian positions in Jammu and Kashmir commences. Pakistani ground forces launch their attack at 0500hrs.
6 September	Operation *Riddle* commences.
7 September	Operation *Nepal* commences.
7–11 September	Battle of Phillora.
8–10 September	Battle of Asal Uttar.
14, 18–19 Sept	Battle of Chawinda.
23 September	Second Indo-Pakistani War ends.

Indian forces examine a recent battlefield in the Lahore sector. As part of the Mutual Defense Assistance Program (MDAP) the upgraded, World War II-vintage 75mm M4A1 Sherman became the M4A1E6 ('E' for 'experimental') with a more powerful 76mm main gun. Under this modernization programme the new tanks incorporated a muzzle brake, gun travel lock, and the capability to use a canvas gun-shield cover, as well as having a field telephone affixed to the hull rear for less-exposed communication with supporting infantry. (© Bettmann/CORBIS)

DESIGN AND DEVELOPMENT

CENTURION

ORIGINS

Conceived to counter the ever more formidable tanks developed by Nazi Germany, the Centurion story began at the height of World War II. At that time British tank doctrine made a distinction between 'infantry' tanks – slow-moving, heavily armoured and intended for infantry support – and fast-moving 'cruiser' tanks designed to exploit a breakthrough and relying upon their mobility to aid their defence. In an effort to address the limitations of the 'cruiser' concept, and related parliamentary and press concerns, in September 1942 Britain's War Office revised its future tank-development policy to address its need for an all-purpose 'universal' tank chassis. Mindful of the fact that the British Government had prohibited the development of projects that could not be put into service by 1944, in July 1943 the War Office entrusted the Department of Tank Design (DTD) – under the energetic, Australian-born engineer Claude D. Gibb – to proceed with developing the 'A41 Heavy Cruiser Tank'. On 7 October 1943 the Director of the Royal Armoured Corps (DRAC), Major-General Raymond Briggs, outlined the proposed vehicle's desired characteristics.

Intended as an improvement over the A34 Comet cruiser tank then in development, the new design was to possess a 650hp (485kW) petrol engine, durability sufficient for at least 4,800km of use, and a turret ring at least equal in diameter to that of the M4 Sherman in order to accommodate a larger main armament, if needed, and thus avoid

A Centurion Mk 7 (42BA25). The turret bins held items such as crew greatcoats, blankets and groundsheets, along with an Oddy (named after its inventor) high-pressure grease pump, a 4-tonne hydraulic lifting jack and a camouflage net. Flat storage containers running along both sides of the hull top held equipment, including shovels, hammers, bleaching powder tins, tent parts, rope and an engine cover. To assist the driver, a pair of small mirrors was positioned at the upper edge of both track guards. The pair of six-tube No. 1 Mk 1 smoke-grenade dischargers fired No. 80 White Phosphorus in sets or salvo out to 60m to provide a short-duration smokescreen. The commander's No. 6 Mk 1 vision cupola comprised seven fixed and one extensible episcopes that provided all-around visibility. A sight and periscopic were also provided, with the cupola rotated via a traverse mechanism or a handwheel after first disengaging the mechanism. The protective metal guards surrounding each 26-volt, 50-watt, double-filament headlight served as protection from foliage during operations. Additional 26-volt, 6-watt lights were affixed atop the track guards forward of the stowage bins to indicate the vehicle's width during poor visibility. (TM 6201-E6, The Tank Museum)

creating a cramped turret. The A41's hull was to weather landmine blasts better than that of previous British tanks, and it was to possess both a high reverse speed for quick repositioning or withdrawal during combat and – responding to a General Staff request of 3 January 1943 – a main armament capable of firing armour-piercing (AP), as well as high-explosive (HE), rounds. Although weapons such as the QF 3.7in (94mm) anti-aircraft gun were available in quantity, because the 17-pdr L/55 anti-tank gun had proven its effectiveness against late-war German armour – especially when mounted in a modified M4 Sherman 'Firefly' turret – the DTD chose it (barring an aborted consideration to use a QF 32-pdr (94mm) cannon). The A41 was also to possess a fighting compartment sufficient for three crewmen, and adequate side protection to counter shape-charged projectiles. However, although its glacis was to be thick enough to resist a high-velocity 8.8cm impact at typical engagement ranges, the commensurate weight increase meant that the A41 would exceed the 36-tonne limit that would enable it to make best use of existing transport trailers and bridges, especially the Bailey varieties, which could be quickly thrown across rivers in the absence of established crossings. The DTD pressured the War Office into rescinding the weight and dimension limitations for using what narrow rail gauges remained in use – and the commonly high station-platform, loading-gauge railcars – with the result that the A41, now weighing in at 39 tonnes, represented the heaviest tank Britain had produced to date.

CENTURION MK 7 SPECIFICATIONS

General

Production: 1953–60

Vehicles produced: 775

Combat weight: 51.62 tonnes

Crew: four (commander, gunner, loader/radio operator, driver)

Dimensions

Hull length / overall: 7.82m / 9.85m

Width (without aprons / with aprons): 3.28m / 3.39m

Height: 3.02m

Ground clearance: 0.51m

Armour (degrees from vertical)

Glacis (upper / lower): 76mm @ 57 degrees / 76mm @ 45 degrees

Hull side: 51mm @ 12 degrees

Hull rear (upper / lower): 32mm @ 7 degrees / 19mm @ 62 degrees

Hull roof (forward / main / rear): 29mm @ 80 degrees / 29mm @ 90 degrees / 10mm @ 90 degrees

Hull bottom: 17mm @ 90 degrees

Turret face: 152mm @ 0 degrees

Turret mantlet: 152mm curved

Turret side (starboard / port upper / port lower): 89mm @ 0 degrees / 51mm @ 60 degrees / 89mm @ 10 degrees

Turret rear (upper / lower): 51mm curved / 89mm @ 0 degrees

Turret roof (forward / main): 51mm @ 73 degrees / 29mm @ 90 degrees

Cupola side: 90mm @ 0 degrees

Skirting plate: 6mm @ 0 degrees

Armament

Main gun: QF 20-pdr (83.8mm) L/67 (64 rounds, typically 50 per cent AP and 50 per cent HE)

Elevation / depression: 20 degrees / 10 degrees

Sight: Mk 1 or Mk 1/1 periscopic (6×)

Secondary: One 303in Browning M1919 A4 MG coaxial (3,600 rounds)

Main gun rate of fire: 4–8rds/min

Turret rotation (360 degrees): 25 seconds @ 3,000 engine rpm

Communications

Internal: Intercom (incorporated in No. 19 WT)

External: No. 19 WT and No. 38 AFV radios

Motive power

Engine: Rolls-Royce Meteor Mk IVB (or Mk IVB/1) 12-cylinder (liquid-cooled) 60-degree vee of 27l (above 80-octane petrol)

Power/weight (net): 635bhp (474kW) (sustained) @ 2,550rpm (9.32kW/tonne)

Transmission: Merritt-Brown Z51R (five forward, two reverse)

Performance

Ground pressure: $0.928kg/cm^2$

Maximum speed (road): 34.6km/h

Operational range (road/ cross country): 190km / 96km

Fuel consumption (road / cross country): 5.45l/km / 10.80l/km

Fording: 1.45m

Step climbing: 0.91m

Climbing, degrees: 35 degrees

Trench crossing: 3.35m

CENTURION MK 7, A SQUADRON, 3RD CAVALRY

Indian Army Centurions retained their original colour, which eventually faded to a flat green. As per the British Army, coloured 'tac' (tactical) signs were often used, into which identically coloured troop numbers were set. These configurations comprised A Squadron (triangle; 1–4 troops); B Squadron (square; 5–8 troops); C Squadron (circle; 9–12 troops); and Regimental HQ (diamond). Squadron numbers further indicated unit seniority, with '1' allocated to the squadron HQ vehicle. Larger formations would often have a special symbol affixed to their tanks' front port track guard, such as 1st Armoured Division's black elephant on a yellow shield, although these were commonly ordered to be obscured prior to action for reasons of security. The vehicle's tactical marking, such as

a black square with a '25' in white, was displayed on the opposite track guard; this number was repeated on the hull rear just above the level of the towing pintle. Vehicle nicknames were provided, with the first letter matching the squadron designation, and with command tanks usually displaying theirs between the glacis headlights. Regimental commanders adopted the names of battle honours, such as 'Chitral' (The Deccan Horse, for the 1895 siege), with The Deccan Horse's regimental commander's tank always being 'Cambrai' for the 1917 battle. Indian Army Centurions possessed a registration number (e.g. KX261) on the lower front hull and track guard stowage bins. To assist aerial Identification Friend or Foe, some Centurions had a pale-yellow solid circle painted on the turret roof.

9.85m

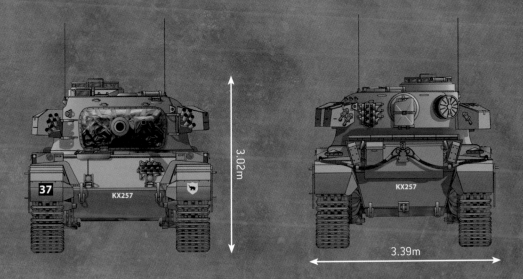

3.02m

3.39m

DEVELOPMENT AND PRODUCTION

To provide overall administration and oversight during the tank-creation process, British policy designated a company possessing the relevant experience and production capacity to act as 'parent'. As the commercial vehicle firm Leyland Motors had previously headed the A27 Cromwell/Centaur projects, and presently that of the A34 Comet, the firm was chosen to lead the A41 programme. With a second facility built at Farington in Lancashire in November 1939, Leyland Motors had further supplied 2,000 Valentine and 1,600 Churchill final drives, and 1,142 Wilson steering units for cruiser tanks. Vickers Ltd (Elswick Works, Newcastle upon Tyne) was similarly tasked as per the General Staff requirements to include Government assets in the process, and the Government's Royal Ordnance Factories (ROF) at Woolwich and Leeds (Barnbow) were to provide vehicle construction. Leyland Motors' subsidiary, the London-based Associated Equipment Company Ltd (AEC) – a producer of commercial and passenger vehicles, heavy goods chassis, and diesel engines – was appointed 'design parent'.

In late May 1944, AEC produced an A41 mock-up hull in mild steel to validate the chosen suspension, engine, transmission and control systems, followed by a second example in armoured steel for stowage and defensive firing trials. Next, 20 A41 prototypes would be constructed at ROF Woolwich and ROF Nottingham (hull and suspension units); the batch comprised five different armament configurations so as to determine optimal weapons complements. In order to counter the effectiveness of German anti-tank guns, and engage unarmoured and lightly armoured targets or infantry in built-up positions, prototype vehicles 1 to 5 were to incorporate a quick-

A Centurion tank being built at ROF Leeds in 1949. The initial run of 100 post-prototype Centurion Mark I (A41*) tanks possessed an OQF 17-pdr (76.2mm) L/55 Mk 6 cannon, with a muzzle brake, and carried 70 rounds. The vehicle also incorporated a 12-tonne hexagonal turret, with two extra rear storage boxes on the sides in lieu of a bustle rack. Following a roughly 13-week construction process, on completion, each Centurion was subjected to component inspection and a host of on- and off-road acceptance trials. The Centurion eventually progressed through 13 marks, with varying upgrades and configurations; both the Centurion Mk III and Mk 7 would be exported to India. (© Hulton-Deutsch Collection/CORBIS)

firing, independently mounted, loader-fired coaxial 20mm Polsten gun; this UK-produced weapon, based on an unfinished Polish simplification of the Swiss Oerlikon cannon, was mounted to the left of the 17-pdr main gun. A rear-firing 7.92mm Besa machine gun, a British version of the Czechoslovak ZB-53 that created a considerable amount of toxic propellant fumes during firing, was incorporated into the turret's rear. Vehicles 6 to 10 were to incorporate an additional optical linkage between the main and secondary guns, and – instead of the Besa – a circular hatch at the turret's rear for removal of the 17-pdr main gun, while vehicles 11 to 15 only substituted a 7.92mm Besa machine gun for the Polsten cannon. The remaining five pilot vehicles (designated A41S) were to have Sinclair 'Powerflow' gearboxes, and sported the Ordnance QF high-velocity 77mm (76.2mm) L/49 main gun found on the Comet. Vehicles 16 to 18 were to incorporate a ball-mounted Besa machine gun in place of the rear turret hatch; 19 and 20 retained the latter, and included provision for a 7.92mm Besa machine gun in the glacis.

In April 1945, ROF Woolwich completed the first A41 prototype, which was delivered to the Fighting Vehicles Proving Establishment for trials. Three more vehicles followed, with the last one sent to the Royal Armoured Corps Gunnery School at Lulworth Camp in Dorset for gunnery trials at month's end. By May prototypes 3, 9 and 11 (ROF Woolwich) and 4, 6 and 8 (ROF Nottingham) had also been completed; these were shipped to Antwerp on 14 May for operational testing, although as the war

A Centurion Mk 7 in British service. To improve on the Mk 5's limited range, a jettisonable external fuel tank was tested, which was later replaced by a 910-litre armoured monowheel fuel-trailer option. Both fuel carriers were eventually eliminated when a third internal fuel tank was incorporated, which increased fuel capacity from 550 litres to 1,036 litres. The deplorable transmission remained, but was made more accessible for maintenance. The bolts that secured the track sections, side skirts and brake drums were found to come loose quickly, and these were replaced by US-designed SAE-threaded bolts. A storage grid was attached to the turret's rear for a camouflage net. (Simon Dunstan)

The Centurion Mk III employed a 20-pdr cannon, with a counterweight affixed to the muzzle to help balance the barrel. This feature reduced weight on the connecting and control components, and facilitated gyrostabilizer movement. (TM 0173-E2, The Tank Museum)

in Europe had already ended, trials were delayed by a few weeks. In Operation *Sentry*, these half-dozen A41s conducted a 630km drive to Gribbohm, Germany, to compare their performance against that of the M4 Sherman and the Cromwell. Gunnery trials at Belgium's Lommel Range followed, and when all planned field tests had been satisfactorily completed the prototypes were shown to other Allied armoured regiments before being returned to Britain in July. Although the crews had endured mechanical problems related to the engine, gearbox and front idler brackets, and found the lengthy Polsten gun to be unwieldy, they otherwise overwhelmingly approved of the A41, deeming it superior to previous British tank designs.

By 1951, Centurion Mk IIs were transitioning to Mk IIIs, following some 250 modifications, including an additional 25mm of turret armour, a new cupola machine gun and antenna mounts, and new engine deck rails. Upgraded to a QF 20-pdr (83.8mm) main gun, the barrel was a Type A variety that had a counterweight instead of a muzzle brake. As had been incorporated into the Centurion Mk II/1, its successor had gyroscopic stabilization equipment for elevation and deflection, which provided far better accuracy due to its fully automatic electromagnetic servo stabilizer, and allowed the gunner to track and engage a target while the tank was moving. Subsequent Mk 5 and Mk 6 versions retained these features (a Mk 4 'Close Support' variety not being produced), as well as a canvas-covered mantlet, and a pair of six-barrel, turret-mounted 51mm smoke-grenade launchers.

Between 1953 and 1960, ROF Leeds and Leyland Motors, operating out of Preston, built 775 of what was arguably the definitive Centurion, the Mk 7 (FV 4012).

Based on the Centurion Mk 5, this new iteration, like the others, lacked a Nuclear, Biological, Chemical (NBC) system and amphibious capabilities, although a deep-fording kit was developed. The Mk 7 also featured new engine deck rails, and a slightly extended rear hull to accommodate an additional fuel tank to improve the tank's limited range. A 20-pdr ammunition loading hatch on the hull's port side offered a degree of protection to supply personnel and crews who could thus avoid unnecessary exposure when on the vehicle; it was accessed by lifting the covering hinged track skirt upwards. Although the Centurion Mk 7 would also be modified with increased glacis plating (Mk 7/1) and a 105mm L7A1 main armament (Mk 7/2), Indian Army vehicles during the 1965 conflict retained the original 20-pdr main gun.

M48 PATTON

ORIGINS

The United States had toyed with a few 'heavy' tank prototypes early in World War II, but the US Army Ground Forces commander, Lieutenant General Lesley McNair, opposed the concept, believing instead that the US M4 Sherman 'medium' tank, initially designed for infantry support, provided an adequate platform on which to incorporate upgrades to maintain battlefield viability. The US Ordnance Department, however, continued to create exploratory designs, with the T26E1 ('T' indicating prototype, and 'E' meaning experimental) presenting perhaps the most successful solution, with its 90mm cannon and 102mm-thick glacis. Fielded in the closing weeks of World War II in Europe, the 42-tonne M26 Pershing ('M' meaning

As the first 'Patton' iteration, the M46 (as evidenced by the tension-compensating idler wheel) incorporated a 90mm M3A1 gun, this being a modified version of the cannon that served the same role as the German 8.8cm anti-aircraft/anti-tank gun during World War II. Depicted during the conflict in Korea, this M3A1 gun has a fume extractor and new muzzle. When Communist North Korean forces suddenly attacked across the peninsula's demilitarized zone in 1950, only the M24 Chaffee light tank was immediately available, as heavier American tanks were barred from driving on and damaging roads in occupied Japan. By the time M4 Shermans and M26 Pershings were allocated to the theatre, US and United Nations forces had been pressed into a constrained perimeter around the south-eastern port city of Pusan. During the fighting, and in the post-Inchon counter-attack, the M26/M46 displayed a marked superiority over the Soviet-provided T-34-85. Ultimately, 1,160 M46s were produced, including 360 that were improved/remanufactured into M46A1s ('A' indicating standardized modification), but in 1952 the improved M47 began replacing its predecessor. (NARA)

standardized) showed promise against heavier German armour, despite being underpowered.

In November 1945 a newly created 'War Department Equipment Board', tasked with overseeing the post-war modernization of the US Army, outlined a five-year programme; much as had happened after 1918, this involved budgetary constraints and considerable force draw-downs. A notable lack of interest within the US automotive industry concerning the development of a satisfactory tank engine meant that the Ordnance Department resorted to modified air-cooled radial aircraft engines. In April 1946, in an attempt to provide service unification as per US President Harry S. Truman's initiative, the Armored Force (including Tank Destroyer Command) and Cavalry were merged as the 'Armored Cavalry'. The next month, the War Department Equipment Board completed its report on US Army material needs, having determined to maintain and improve the existing M24 Chaffee, M4 Sherman and M26 Pershing designs, and to avoid an immediate transition to new alternatives. In November 1946 the Armored Center was revived; in response to a growing Soviet/Communist threat in Korea, Eastern Europe and elsewhere, military leadership looked to more modern T37 (light), T42 (medium) and T43 (heavy) tank prototype solutions, with emphasis on several factors, including light weight, manoeuvrability, parts standardization, reliability, ease of maintenance and conservation of materials – and mounting the largest main gun possible.

When the US Government suddenly found itself without any tanks in production, nor anything capable of adequately contesting newer tank models the Soviets had produced and distributed to friendly nations, a frenzied production atmosphere that mirrored that of 1940–41 resulted in testing and development cycles frequently occurring simultaneously, and often without adequate pre-production evaluation. As per the Army Organization Act of 1950, armour was officially deemed a permanent US Army branch, and the rebuilt M26 Pershing, with its new cross-drive transmission, bore evacuator, fire control and an improved suspension, was rechristened as an interim M46 Medium (aka General Patton) Tank.

Featuring a T42 medium tank prototype's turret atop an M46 hull, and adding a 90mm gun that could be fired by the commander or gunner, the M47 continued the tradition of having an underpowered, fuel-inefficient engine, in addition to a complex and fragile stereoscopic rangefinder, and a regularly malfunctioning turret-control system. As a short-term fix to a potentially long-term problem, the manoeuvrable M47 suffered from a poor rangefinder and an inadequate 90mm ammunition-storage arrangement – only 11 rounds were slated for the turret – but it provided the basis for (and insights into) a more combat-suitable successor. On 6 January 1951, President Truman ordered the institution of a new US $500-million tank-procurement programme as the next step to bringing this replacement to fruition.

DEVELOPMENT AND PRODUCTION

Having produced roughly 25 per cent of the 89,568 American tanks made during World War II – including the M3 and M4 – the US Government-owned Detroit Arsenal Tank Plant (DATP) in Warren, Michigan, had the necessary infrastructure and expertise to enable it to continue such duties after 1945. In October 1950, DATP began considering the third Patton iteration, even before it began to produce the M47

(3,443 M47s would be produced in 1952–54). Two months later, the facility was awarded a letter of intent to develop six T48 prototypes and 542 M48 production models, which were to serve as the opening batch of a total of 9,000 to be produced by mid-1954. On 27 February 1951, the Ordnance Technical Committee Minutes (OTCM) No. 33791 initiated the design of the new tank, designated the '90mm Gun Tank T48', which (with the hull machine-gunner position removed) required a four-man crew – a first for an American medium tank. In March 1951, before the prototypes had been completed, the Fisher Body Division of the General Motors Corporation and the Ford Motor Company at Livonia, Michigan were each given an M48 production contract. To complete such an ambitious project on time, corners were occasionally cut, which resulted in considerable teething problems with the engine, transmission, suspension and tracks. Anticipating such problems, integration committees comprising military and industrial representatives were established to coordinate tank and component development, and to provide early defect warnings and fix recommendations.

Under Chrysler's direction, work commenced by the end of 1951 on what would be an entirely new design, and not a derivative of the M26 Pershing. Although retaining the M47's petrol engine and cross-drive transmission, the M48 featured improved armour protection via an elliptical hull and a one-piece cast hemispherical turret for better ballistic protection, a fire-control system with rangefinder and ballistic computer and drive, and an upgraded suspension. In December 1951, the first prototype was built, and three months later Chrysler began producing M48s at its Delaware Tank Plant in Newark, New Jersey. On 1 July 1952 the M48 was officially given its 'Patton' nickname, and on 2 April 1953, OTCM No. 34765 standardized the last of the Patton-series tanks as the '90mm Gun Tank M48 Patton'. Meeting this goal, however, required that production occur simultaneously with operational testing and development. Chrysler Corporation, being the tank's principal producer, sought to satisfy this requirement in a manner reminiscent of M3 medium tank production during World War II, by constructing a new tank plant in Newark, where M48s would be built while the company continued to evolve the design.

Despite shortages of materials, mobilization-control agency officials attempted to satisfy material needs, and to minimize disrupting the US economy by over-burdening business and fuelling inflation as a result of a dearth of products. Because estimating

M48 PATTON SPECIFICATIONS

General

Production: 1952–53

Vehicles produced: 4,392

Combat weight: 47.62 tonnes

Crew: four (commander, gunner, loader, driver)

Dimensions

Hull length / overall / with fuel tank kit: 6.97m / 8.81m / 10.5m

Width: 3.63m

Height: 3.09m

Ground clearance: 0.42m

Armour (degrees from vertical)

Glacis (upper / lower): 110mm @ 60 degrees / 102mm @ 35 degrees tapering to 61mm @ 53 degrees

Hull side (upper / lower): 76mm @ 0 degrees / 90mm curved

Hull rear (upper / lower): 35mm @ 30 degrees / 25mm @ 60 degrees

Hull roof (forward / rear): 57mm @ 90 degrees / 20mm and 25mm @ 90 degrees

Hull bottom (forward / middle / rear): 38mm @ 90 degrees / 32mm @ 90 degrees / 13mm @ 90 degrees

Turret face: 178mm @ 30 degrees

Turret mantlet: 114mm @ 30 degrees

Turret side (starboard / port upper / port lower): 76mm @ 12 degrees / 65mm @ 33 degrees / 115mm @ 28 degrees

Turret rear: 51mm curved

Turret roof: 25mm @ 90 degrees

Armament

Main gun: 90mm Gun M41 in Mount M87 (60 rounds, typically 50 per cent AP and 50 per cent HE)

Elevation / depression: 20 degrees / 10 degrees

Sight: M20 periscope (1×/6×)

Secondary: One .50-calibre MG HB M2 in cupola mount (1,360 rounds); one .30-calibre MG 37 coaxial (5,950 rounds)

Main gun rate of fire: 8rds/min

Turret rotation (360 degrees): 15 seconds @ 2,800 engine rpm

Communications

Internal: Four stations plus external extension kit AN/VIA-1 interphone

External: AN/GRC-3 to -8 series or AN/VRC-7 radios

Motive power

Engine: Continental AV-1790-5B 12-cylinder, four-cycle, 90-degree vee, fuel injection (air-cooled) 29.36l (80-octane petrol)

Power/weight (net): 704bhp (525kW) (sustained) @ 2,800rpm (23.19kW/tonne)

Transmission: Cross-drive CD-850-4A or CD-850-4B (two forward; one reverse)

Performance

Ground pressure: 0.84kg/cm²

Maximum speed (road): 48km/h

Operational range (road / cross-country): 115km / 60km

Fuel consumption (road / cross country): 6.6l/km / 12.6l/km

Fording: 1m

Step climbing: 0.91m

Climbing, degrees: 60 degrees

Trench crossing: 2.6m

M48 PATTON, B SQUADRON, 24TH CAVALRY

Pakistani M48 Pattons sported an overall olive-drab paint scheme that over time faded to a green-grey. To provide a degree of camouflage to better match the battlefield terrain, wet sand or mud was often smeared over the turret and hull. Two-digit turret numbers in Urdu provided vehicle identification, and were either white or a red base colour with white edging to assist visual contrast. A serial number was occasionally applied to the hull stowage-box sides, hull, and rear. Like their Indian Army armoured counterparts,

Pakistan Armoured Corps divisional insignia, such as a mailed fist on a two-colour square (1st Armoured Division) was usually removed during combat operations for reasons of security. One, two or three barrel bands likely indicated A, B and C squadrons within the particular battalion, the number of which was on the turret. Considering the M48's limited operational range a jettison fuel tank kit was provided; this added 100km and could be cable-released prior to combat.

10.5m

3.09m

3.63m

An M48 from Task Force 'Razor' moves across Death Valley, California on 22 April 1955 during a 270km tactical armoured march. On reaching their destination – Camp Desert Rock, Nevada – these vehicles will subsequently be used in the US Army's first atomic armoured manoeuvre at Yucca Flat. As part of the complement of sandbagged trenches, aircraft and vehicles to be tested during the 'Apple-2' detonation on 5 May 1955, M48 crews were to turn off their engines, 'button up' and rotate their turrets away from ground zero. Following the 29kT blast, these tanks 'attacked' towards the resulting mushroom cloud to mimic fighting in such an environment. Note the pads to protect the road from track damage. (© Bettmann/CORBIS)

requirements for materials and designing production schedules were difficult and complex tasks, the military departments initially determined the numbers and types of end items to be acquired. In part based on manufacturer-provided information, the services translated these figures into material quantities needed for production. With the help of contractor input, the US services created time-phased production schedules that endeavoured to square desired delivery dates with manufacturing capabilities. The Munitions Board then forwarded the military departments' estimates of raw-materials requirements and the relevant production schedules to the mobilization-control agencies for resource allocation. Aggravated by a post-1945 lack of accounting personnel, a series of worker strikes and a degree of 'scope creep', difficulties in obtaining machine tools caused the greatest delay to Patton tank production during the early 1950s. In mid-1951, as the US rearmament programme ramped up, shortages of raw materials became apparent, including steel, aluminium, chromium, molybdenum and nickel.

Most contemporary tank turrets narrowed at their base, creating a shot trap between the lower turret and hull that increased vulnerability. The M48 design eliminated this weakness, since the turret base overhung the tracks. The turret's shape derived from that of the Soviet IS-3 heavy tank, considered the nemesis of American tanks in the late 1940s and early 1950s because of its superior armour, armament and range. The US Army's emphasis upon long-range accuracy led to the incorporation of a fire-control system, which included a stereoscopic rangefinder, ballistic computer, ballistic drive and gunner's periscope. Essentially smaller versions of their naval equivalents, they enabled tanks to engage effectively at much greater ranges than in World War II – a critical consideration for an army expecting to enter the battlefield outnumbered. Instead of a gunner's sight slaved to the gun tube, the ballistic computer and drive computed the range and elevated the gun; this meant the gunner's job was eased, as all he had to do was keep the crosshairs on the target. The mechanical ballistic computer made a more accurate computation of range possible by mathematically accounting for such factors as vehicle cant and ammunition type.

The first M48 production tanks suffered from excessive oil consumption, hydraulic fluid fires resulting from turret penetrations and – after a few hundred kilometres of use – engine failures. The petrol engine managed only 6.6l/km, which with small internal fuel tanks limited range to just 115km over roads. The M48's width proved too great for many European tunnels, thus complicating rail transport. Operational readiness rates of M48-equipped units tended to be low. The tank suffered from engine, transmission, track and suspension problems, and the fire-control system's complexity made it difficult to operate. However, the M48 was considered an even match for its Soviet T-54/55 counterpart, although the glacis of the older IS-3 proved tougher to penetrate.

The M48 remained in production from 1952 to 1959, with 11,703 tanks built in total. With the M48 having proven a generally successful design, improvements and changes were incorporated, such as an enclosed cupola (M48A1), and an improved engine and transmission, and turret control (M48A2). Starting in 1959 most M48s were upgraded to M48A3s, with a final M48A5 iteration incorporating a 105mm gun. The M48 served with US forces in Vietnam where it provided excellent infantry support, and along with Royal Australian Armoured Corps Centurion tanks proved particularly mine-resistant. Exported to a variety of NATO and US-friendly nations, the M48 fought in the Indo-Pakistani wars of 1965 and 1971 with Pakistani forces and in the Middle East with Israeli forces. The M48 was replaced in US service by the M60.

In order to get the T48 into service quickly as the M48, prototype testing was curtailed, with many M47 components retained, such as the cylindrical blast deflector. Other components, such as the auxiliary tensioning idler, were removed. This iteration featured an open cupola that provided the theoretical capability for anti-aircraft fire, but the pintle-mounted .50-calibre machine gun was better suited to suppression and infantry support. An enclosed cupola was subsequently provided to better protect the commander during the machine gun's operation. (TM 7485-F3, The Tank Museum)

TECHNICAL
SPECIFICATIONS

ARMOUR

Having evolved from simple boilerplate protection for World War I armoured vehicles to bolting and riveting steel, and face-hardening – where coal gas was applied to a heated plate's face to harden its exterior while keeping the interior flexible – advances in metallurgy, casting and electric welding facilitated the joining of thicker plate needed for the increasingly heavy armoured vehicles produced during World War II. With steel essentially being iron infused with a small amount of carbon as a hardening agent, the right balance needed to be maintained: too much carbon promoted tensile strength at the expense of ductility, weldability and toughness, while too little reduced impact resistance. To impart additional characteristics to the steel, equally small amounts of other non-ferrous elements could be incorporated, including molybdenum, which being non-oxidizing prevented the introduction of unwanted oxygen into the molten steel, and added hardness by increasing high-temperature tensile qualities and creep strength to minimize deformation. Molybdenum was often used in conjunction with chromium, which improved carburization, abrasion and wear resistance, and promoted uniformity during tempering, as the core of thick armour cooled and heated at different rates to that of its surface. Elements like copper could also be included to help resist corrosion.

Throughout World War II most heavy armour plate was rolled or cast homogeneous, and comprised nickel-chromium-molybdenum alloyed steel. Emphasis was placed upon internal uniformity to minimize structural weakness and integrity loss during an impact; once sufficiently heated, the molten steel was poured into ingots, which after cooling were removed, reheated and rolled in order to create the desired thickness and force the metal's ferrite (iron) grains to align, and further promote or alter strength, ductility and toughness. Nickel-chrome-molybdenum alloyed steel possessed a tensile strength that required a force of between 9,840 and 11,200kg/cm^2 to fail structurally; its Brinell Hardness Number (BHN) of around 300 was within the 260 to 300 range generally considered a good compromise between soft and hard tank armour. This steel was under the 375+ BHN threshold that required special hardened cutting tools; plate density was between 7,700 and 8,030kg/m^3. With armour 'hardness' dependent primarily on the alloy and heat treatment, rolling reduced the grain size, and commensurately promoted strength. This quality helped redirect sufficient energy against the incoming round to make it shatter or deform on impact, which in turn diffused or deflected its kinetic energy, and maintained plate integrity by spreading the impacting energy over as large an area as possible.

CENTURION

While sloped armour plate increased its effective thickness, and promoted off-angle impacts, its primary use was to minimize the tank's targeted cross-section toward the

Soldiers from the Pakistan Army's 25th Cavalry examine a captured Indian Army Centurion Mk 7 fitted with a Type B barrel, following the fighting near Gadgor on 11 September 1965. Because of the size and weight of the Centurion's hull, large jigs and rotary manipulators were used during welding to position the joints vertically and so make the job less fatiguing, and to reduce the number of electrode runs. In contrast, welding the tank's side skirts proved particularly difficult due to warping and stress fractures. In an effort to reduce such manufacturing defects or irregularities, X-ray machines were incorporated into the inspection process. (bharat-rakshak.com)

turret, this generally being the vehicle's most exposed part, and commensurately possessing the most armour. While the Centurion Mk I possessed a partially cast turret with a welded roof set into a 1.88m-diameter turret ring, subsequent iterations sported a turret that had been machined from an 8.25-tonne casting.

Although both the Centurion Mk 7 and the M48 possessed similar homogeneous armor/metallurgical compositions, the Centurion's preponderance of flat plate provided a comparable strength modifier over its adversary's cast armour in a direct thickness comparison. While cast armour allowed for the construction of a variety of curved turret and hull configurations, and helped minimize the area vulnerable to a direct impact, a solid strike was more likely to achieve penetration than against plate that had been rolled to promote grain alignment, and thus strength. Travelling at 912m/sec, the 90mm M318A1 APCBC round used by the Pakistanis could penetrate 160mm of Rolled Homogeneous Armour (RHA) at 100m, 135mm at 1,000m and about 110mm at 2,000m. The M304 HVAP projectile provided even greater penetrative capabilities: 255mm at 100m, 199mm at 1,000m and 156mm at 2,000m. While HEAT rounds, such as the M431, achieved even greater penetrations, their rather limited, unobstructed 1,000-metre range limited battlefield options, while side plates, as on the Centurion, served to prematurely trigger the round's explosive molten jet, which subsequently lacked the proper form or penetrative capabilities.

Indian Army personnel examine damage to an M48 Patton at 'Patton-Nagar' ('Patton City'). The M48 Patton's glacis had a BHN of 210, which being relatively soft minimized spall, although a non-overmatching round ('overmatching' meaning to have a diameter greater than the impacted plate's thickness) was more likely to achieve penetration due to the added 'grip' when compared to harder armour, which was more likely to deflect such a round. (Simon Dunstan)

M48

In addition to RHA plates, casting provided for curved armoured surfaces, which, although typically weaker, provided for a variety of configurations which RHA could not accommodate. During the late 1930s the Ford Company successfully experimented with a mixture of cast iron and steel alloyed with copper, chromium and silicon. The firm was tasked with producing armoured vehicles during World War II, including the M4 Sherman, so it was natural that the firm would continue such manufacturing in the post-war years, such as with the M48 Patton. Considering the M48 hull's large size and complexity, finding a suitable manufacturing facility initially proved difficult, but the Lima Locomotive Works (Lima-Hamilton after 1947) in Ohio was eventually selected to cast the hull as complete upper and lower sections, with openings to accommodate for suspension components, hatches, engine access ports and the like.

With the M48 having retained the T43's 2.16m-diameter turret ring, which incorporated a 120mm gun, the use of a smaller 90mm cannon in the M48 allowed for smoothly tapering turret walls that eliminated the shot traps found on the M47, save for at the rear and under the mantlet. Like the hull, the turret was cast from homogeneous steel that provided a tensile strength of 3,772.95kg/cm², with the same 300 BNH found on the Centurion. As casting lacked the strength-inducing rolling process of flat plate, the M48 was not as resilient against 20-pdr HEAT rounds as the British tank was to 90mm equivalents – a feature accentuated by the Centurion's side skirts.

ARMAMENT

CENTURION

As a quick-firing weapon, the QF 20-pdr L/64 was designed to rapidly fire AP and medium HE rounds, in which the propellant charges were loaded into a brass case that sealed the breech to prevent expanding propellant gas from escaping. Early examples of the gun featured Type A barrels with a counterbalance at the muzzle, while after 1956 a Type B 'muzzle swelling' barrel was introduced, which incorporated a fume extractor onto which barrel-balancing counterweights were welded; the Indian Army Centurions operating in 1965 all appeared to have the Type B barrel. Changes also were made to the depression stop rail around the rear deck, and to the barrel travelling clamp. The gun's Metro-Vickers (Metrovick) stabilizer depended on available power to compensate for any frequency and vibration disruptions, such as during vehicle movement.

The Centurion Mk 7's Metrovick Firing Vehicle Gunnery Control Equipment (FVGCE) enabled the 20-pdr cannon to remain fixed on a target while the vehicle was moving – something that made inserting a round into the breech rather more difficult than when stationary, although it was very effective when firing HE rounds or machine guns. The gunner's Mk 1 or Mk 1/1 periscopic sight provided 6× magnification, which together allowed with the FVGCE the gunner to target a moving vehicle, fire quickly and address the next target. Such actions, however, came at a price in terms of the rate of fire while engaging in straight (five or six rounds per minute) or zigzag (four rounds per minute) movement, compared to being stationary (eight rounds per minute).

CENTURION AMMUNITION

Painted to minimize corrosion, tank rounds were coloured to distinguish types, with the Centurion's rimmed cartridges retaining a brass finish. The addition of yellow bands to standard-looking projectiles indicated a practice round. The APDS Mk 1 (**1**) projectile was black, with a red stripe to respectively indicate shot and explosive element. It comprised a solid, high tensile steel round including a copper cap to improve penetration by turning the round's tip into the hard impacted area, and an aluminium ballistic cap. On firing the sabot, its restraining nylon slip ring broke to allow its constituent parts to fall away, while the slug continued toward the target at 602m/sec. A No. 410 Mk 1 instantaneous fuse detonated the projectile's explosive mix of RDX and TNT.

The yellow steel high-explosive round (**2**) comprised a No. 410 Mk 2/2 fuse and an RDX/TNT explosive. To indicate the explosive was susceptible to high temperatures during storage a red band was added near the nose. The round had a muzzle velocity of 600m/sec.

Prior to loading the smoke round (**3**), the operator would use a key with a range scale to turn the fuse cone. When fired at 251m/sec and the fuse burnt for the required distance, a charge would fire three smoke generating canisters out the base of the round; these fell to the ground, creating a curtain of smoke. 'WMT' on the cartridge indicated a cordite propellant.

The APDS Mk 3 (**4**) comprised a sub-calibre tungsten steel bolt fitted with an alloy sabot to make up a full-bore round. On firing, the plastic band holding its 'petals' together broke to allow them to fall away, with the slug, with its smaller aerodynamic cross-section, continuing ahead. Such a design imparted roughly the same energy as a full-sized round, while providing a tracer for visually following the trajectory. As loose sabot connections impeded initial stability on firing, the accuracy of such projectiles degraded at longer distances, and although superior penetrators compared to standard AP and APC projectiles, APDS varieties were subsequently less effective at impact angles over 45 degrees.

The 580 steel pellets found in the 20-pdr canister round (**5**) were ideal for engaging localized anti-personnel targets and clearing obstructions, such as dense shrubbery. Its muzzle velocity of 915m/sec enabled a conical range of some 250m.

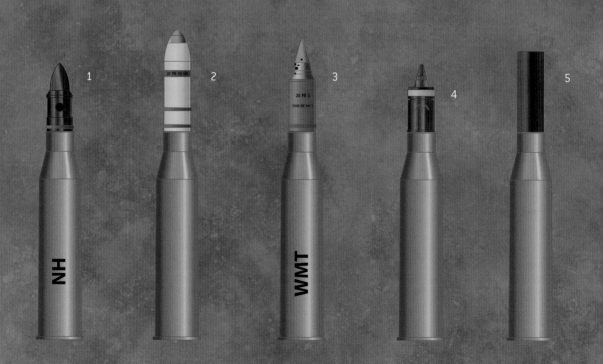

M48 AMMUNITION

The hollow steel forged projectile of the M71A1 (**1**), an HE-T round, was employed for blast and fragmentation against personnel and *matériel*. The round included a boat-tailed base, and a three-second XM10 tracer that was triggered by exploding propellant. A point-detonating M51A5 or M557 fuse triggered a 1kg of Composition B (RDX and TNT) or TNT into a fragmentation blast. Its M19 or M19B1 cartridge case contained an M1 propelling charge, which imparted a muzzle velocity of 730m/sec, and a 15,800m maximum range.

The M318A1 (**2**), an AP-T round, had a conical aluminium windshield to improve ballistics for the underlying hardened solid steel slug. Relying on kinetic energy to penetrate armour, the projectile incorporated a red, rear-mounted, M13, M5A2 or M5A2B1 tracer for visually following the projectile to the target. It used an M108 or M108B1 cartridge, with an 3.9kg propelling charge providing a muzzle velocity of 851m/sec and a maximum range of 21,400m.

Effectively a giant shotgun shell, the cylindrical M336 canister round (**3**) contained a heavy curved steel base behind some 1,281 steel pellets, totalling 6.76kg and some 17 per cent of the projectile's weight. As an antipersonnel round, on firing, air pressure and centrifugal force ruptured its four axial slits to produce a conical spray out to about

183m. The M108B1 cartridge case held M2 propellant that produced a muzzle velocity of 858m/sec. Unlike rounds that remained intact along their trajectory, it was expressly forbidden to fire canister over friendly soldiers.

The projectile of the M332A1 (**4**), an HVAP-T round, comprised a hard tungsten carbide steel core held within an aluminium outer shell, with an alloy windshield to improve ballistics, and an M5A2B1 tracer. An M17 propelling charge was held within an M19 or M19B1 cartridge case which, acting on a physically smaller slug than the M318A1, imparted a muzzle velocity of 1,165m/sec and a maximum range of 14,456m. On impact the outer shell collapsed, and the core penetrated the target.

The M313 smoke round (**5**) was used for marking targets, screening and providing incendiary fires. The projectile included a M15 or M6 propelling charge, within an M19 or M19B1 cartridge case. It relied on a threaded, point-detonating M48A3 or M57 fuse, and an M2 burster initiator that triggered a central M24 Tetrytol bursting charge. This dispensed 0.9kg of white phosphorus, which produced smoke and flaming particles on air contact. It had a muzzle velocity of 821m/sec, and a maximum range of 17,717m.

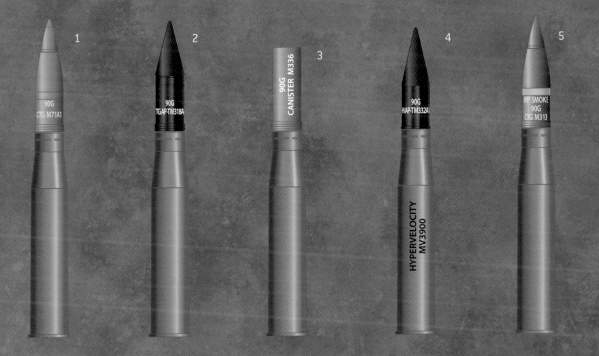

1   2   3   4   5

90G CTG M71A1 — 90G TGAP-TM318A — 90G CANISTER M336 — 90G HAP-TM332A1 — WP SMOKE 90G CTG M313 — HYPERVELOCITY MV3900

The Centurion Mk 7's .303in Browning M1919A4 machine gun was mounted coaxially to the main gun's port side. It was used against enemy infantry and soft targets well within the 20-pdr's combat range to support nearby friendly forces or to help provide a degree of local security for the tank. As tanks would probably not operate without attached infantry and engineers, a large armoured vehicle such as the Centurion provided protection against small-arms fire and shrapnel, as well as being an imposing presence. Given that tanks also tended to draw commensurately greater fire, supporting formations needed to be aware of the risk and avoid clustering against the tank during combat. Because it was positioned higher up than a bow machine gun fitted into the glacis, the M1919A4 could be operated in hull-down defensive positions in concert with the main gun.

M48

Although it was never well regarded in terms of its accuracy or power – a reputation extending back to the M36 Jackson tank destroyer – the 90mm Gun M41 in Mount M87 incorporated into the M48 was an improvement on the M26 Pershing's M3 cannon; it included features of the M3A1 (new muzzle brake and fume extractor) and the M3A2 (metallurgically improved breech ring) found on the M26A1 and M46 Patton. The subsequent T119 experimental variety was developed especially for tanks, with increased chamber pressure, a fume extractor and a new muzzle brake for the T42. Modified for mass production, the M36 (T119E1) was used with the M47, while the lighter, 4.91m-long, semi-automatic M41 (T139) in an M87 mount offered a quicker (15-minute) barrel change for use with the M48, due to it being attached to the breech with interrupted threads. A T48 cylindrical blast deflector was incorporated on early-production M48s, although it – and several other muzzle brakes – were tested to better reduce the amount of dust kicked up during firing, with a T-shaped deflector subsequently chosen.

As with the Centurion, the M48's .30-calibre MG 73 machine gun was located to port, and coaxially with the main gun; it was used to engage infantry and soft targets. A .50-calibre MG HB M2 was located in a flexible cupola mount where it provided a degree of anti-aircraft defense at low altitudes, and could be fired with the commander's hatch closed, although it needed to be externally loaded. The weapon's 890m/sec bullet meant the system could engage area and point targets, including light armoured vehicles, out to some 1,800m and 1,500m respectively. In a defensive role the .50-calibre machine gun could provide bivouac, assembly position and reconnaissance support.

MOBILITY

Considering the rather underdeveloped nature of Jammu and Kashmir's road network beyond larger urban areas, traffic – especially heavy vehicles, such as tanks – and rain could considerably hamper movement, especially when terrain, or the area's soft farmland and waterways, limited off-road alternatives. With the September 1965 fighting occurring at the tail end of the region's July and August rainy season, the weather's impact was minimal – but excessive dust could overwhelm air filters and reduce engine life. Although Punjab's autumn sugar-cane harvesting was several weeks

away, the 3–4m-tall plants presented a visual obstruction – something Indian Army Centurion crews would exploit during the Asal Uttar fighting east of Lahore. In an effort to occupy forward positions or relocate, movement by night offered a reasonably effective solution to help evade enemy ground and air observation, although a lack of night-fighting equipment, especially for the Indians, hampered progress.

In addition to the terrain and environment, Indian and Pakistani tank movements suffered due to incomplete crew training, and a lack of large-scale operational experience among their commanders. During combat, feelings of isolation could reduce a tank crew's effectiveness and make them unnecessarily vigilant and distracted; given the war's short duration, command, control and coordination within formations larger than a battalion or regiment were frequently inconsistent. Such factors meant combat presented the risk of a piecemeal commitment that could be countered more easily and effectively than a concentrated, well-executed movement.

CENTURION
Developed during World War II for Britain's increasingly heavy armoured fighting vehicles, Rolls-Royce's V-12 27-litre Meteor engine was adapted from the company's famous Merlin aero engine. It was stripped of its supercharger, reduction gear and other equipment to make it more compact and simpler to produce; and several modifications, such as modifying the fan drive and full-flow oil filter, and increasing the oil pump's capacity, raised output to between 462 and 470kW. Larger main jets and chokes to the carburettor, roller rockers and a modified magneto advance increased power on the Meteor Mk 4B/1 to 485kW. When the main engine was turned off, an innovative Morris engine provided auxiliary power for the batteries, radios and turret-traverse and -control mechanisms, and for heating food and tea.

Because the Royal Navy had priority on diesel fuel, and the RAF on high-octane fuel, the Army was by default reliant on lower-octane pool petrol. Although this petrol was less flammable and more commonly available than diesel, and allowing for the comparatively smaller engine sizes, it was also less fuel-efficient, which translated into a very short (80km) operational road range. As the Centurion's fuel tanks were mounted astride the engine, a fire bulkhead separated the section from the turret and crew. Supplementing the internal fuel tanks by mimicking the rear-mounted external fuel tanks found on Soviet tanks was found to be unpopular and presented an unnecessary risk due to potential accidents.

The Centurion's transmission was a simple steering and brake-mechanism combination that had proven itself on the Cromwell and Comet, and provided maximum power transfer to the vehicle's rear drive sprockets. This system increased torque and thus mobility over rough terrain, and allowed for spinning on the vehicle's axis instead of a turning radius. A major difference was that the version fitted to the Centurion included a high-speed reverse gear that provided just over 12km/h, and an automatic differential lock.

M48

The M48 initially incorporated the same Continental AV-1790-5B engine as used in the M46A1 and M47. In November 1952 the upgraded AV-1790-7 entered production, followed in August 1954 by the AV-1790-7B. Coupled to an 8-cylinder

The Centurion Mk 7's 607mm-wide tracks comprised 109 cast manganese steel links; in an effort to minimize damaging surfaced roads, rubber pads ('hush puppies') were fitted, although these promoted skidding. The A41's modified Sydney Horstmann suspension relied upon three external hull hardpoints per side, each comprised of two double-wheels – much like the horizontal volute components found on later M4 Shermans. The forward bogie set was farther apart than the others, and the lead and rear road-wheel units included a specialized shock absorber. Along with six return rollers, drive sprockets were at the rear, near the engine, and short spoke idlers at the front, which further facilitated maintenance. (TM 6201-F1, The Tank Museum)

While the tension-adjusting idler near the rear sprocket had been removed on the T48 and early-production M48 models, it was later restored to help minimize the tank's tendency to throw its tracks. The drivetrain retained its predecessor's arrangement of six paired, rubberized steel road wheels, each with an improved independent horizontal torsion bar and vibration dampers, with a seventh acting as the forward-mounted idler. Each track comprised 79 links incorporating a new centre guide, and deeper, rubber-backed steel shoes.
(TM 2621-A5, The Tank Museum)

'Little Joe' engine, the initial powerpack was prone to catching fire when the turret was penetrated and the hydraulic lines ruptured, spewing hydraulic fluid (nicknamed 'cherry juice' because of its red colour) at high pressure into the crew compartment, often producing a fireball due to its very low (150 degrees Celsius) flashpoint.

The M48's suspension included six independently sprung dual-track road wheels per side, each attached to a torsion bar, with the forward two pairs and the rear two pairs of road wheels each having a shock absorber. Considering the vehicle's weight, this type of suspension had historically offered a relatively smooth ride and a reliable framework for medium armoured vehicles, such as the German Panther, in which each rod twisted laterally to allow for the terrain, while not being too loose. Five dual-track return rollers were also affixed to each side, along with an 11-tooth rear drive wheel. The M48 driver controlled the vehicle via a mechanical, aircraft-style steering wheel, as opposed to the stick control found on the M46 and M47. The M48's transmission comprised a General Motors' Cross-drive CD-850-4A or CD-850-4B that provided two forward and one reverse gear, while a 757-litre fuel capacity translated into a very limited operational range – a deficiency corrected in subsequent vehicle iterations. During travel, the M48's main gun was usually kept locked in the cradle; while the steel track guards were prone to snagging and deforming on foliage, and especially barbed wire.

THE COMBATANTS

A SHARED HERITAGE

During World War II, the British Indian Army (as with the forces of other Commonwealth countries) served in the Middle Eastern and Far Eastern theatres. The careers of four regiments, two of which (The Guides Cavalry and Prince Albert Victor's Own Cavalry) would enter Pakistani service in 1947 and two (The Poona Horse and 16th Light Cavalry) that would fight for India in 1965, serve to illustrate the range of locations and tasks performed by the Indian Armoured Corps in 1939–45.

An M5 Stuart light tank of 7th Light Cavalry in Burma on 27 April 1945, during the Allied advance on Rangoon. Although the M5's 37mm main armament was outdated as an anti-tank gun on the contemporary European battlefield, the dearth of Japanese armoured vehicles and the commonly close engagement ranges in the forested and jungle terrain of the Far East meant it was of little handicap in that theatre. The vehicle's light weight made it ideal for infantry support, reconnaissance and spearhead operations. By the start of the 1965 Indo-Pakistani War, the M5 Stuart had been removed from Indian Army service in favour of the more powerful M4 Sherman, AMX-13 and Centurion Mk 7 tanks. (© IWM IND 4652)

33

A pair of Sikh crewmen test the radio atop their early-production, British-provided M4A2(75) Sherman in March 1944 in Iraq. Having traded up from the M3 Grant in November 1943, The Scinde Horse (14th Prince of Wales's Own Cavalry) – serving with 31st Indian Armoured Division – was slated for the Italian campaign, but was instead transferred to Iraq. This A Squadron tank possessed 'dry' ammunition storage, which unlike later 'wet' housings made the rounds susceptible to catastrophic detonation from incoming-round impacts on the hull. The turret includes an early 'split hatch' rotatable commander's cupola, which included a periscope, and a lockable port for mounting a .50-calibre or .30-calibre machine gun. A simple vertical vane (far left) aided the commander in aiming the turret in azimuth when conducting indirect fire, while an armour-covered ventilator and a spotlight fitting are also visible. As an aside, both men hail from the Amritsar region, the scene of heavy fighting in 1965. (© IWM K 6697)

In 1941, The Guides Cavalry – a light reconnaissance regiment operating wheeled armoured vehicles – was posted to Iraq to participate in the Anglo-Soviet invasion of Iran to secure the region's oil production; the regiment was subsequently sent to North Africa in mid-1942 to support the British Eighth Army's retreat. In November 1943, it proceeded to India, where it was converted into an Armoured Car Regiment for operations on the North West Frontier. Prince Albert Victor's Own Cavalry (11th Frontier Force) similarly operated in Syria and Iran before moving to participate in the 1942 Gazala fighting, in which the Axis forces captured the port city of Tobruk and drove the British into Egypt. Subsequently transferred to Burma, the Indian regiment fought the Japanese, and would be allocated to Pakistan in 1947.

Unlike its contemporaries that had transitioned to mechanized forces, The Poona Horse (17th Queen Victoria's Own Cavalry) retained its horses, and performed reconnaissance duties in Iraq; in 1942 the unit served in North Africa before returning to Iraq, and ended the war on Cyprus. In early 1945, 16th Light Cavalry operated in Burma, where it covered over 5,000km from Quetta to the banks of the Irrawaddy River in just three weeks to help eliminate the Japanese presence in the British colony. During 1944, 255th (Indian) Tank Brigade moved to India's Imphal Plain, where it similarly assisted in a major Japanese defeat before serving alongside 16th Light Cavalry during the Irrawaddy River crossing.

On 30 June 1947 a Division Council headed by the recently appointed Viceroy of India, Rear Admiral Lord Mountbatten of Burma, undertook the division of military resources of what had been the British Indian Army. With the Muslim League and Indian National Congress in attendance, 36 per cent of personnel, as well as six armoured, eight artillery and eight infantry regiments, were allocated to Pakistan, with several facilities in India subsequently relocated. All three command training centres were within India's new borders, as were 39 of 46 training establishments, and 14 of 17 ordnance factories.

FORGING A NEW ARMOURED CORPS

INDIA

In large measure due to India retaining a much greater proportion of post-Partition military assets in 1947, the Indian Army benefited from inheriting divisional- and brigade-level command structures in which to organize what was a mix of armoured vehicle types and vintages. At the beginning of the 1950s the Indian Army's armoured units were equipped with older, mechanically unreliable M4 Shermans and also M3A3 Stuart light tanks, the latter of which as far back as 1944 had garnered the moniker of an 'atrocity on tracks' and were thus allocated to reconnaissance and other duties. Although neighbouring Pakistan could put considerably fewer forces and equipment in the field, its steady build-up of arms and its threatening posture regarding Jammu and Kashmir warranted that India similarly keep pace in an effort to provide sufficient conventional forces to defend its lengthy border against this and other threats, such as from China. The 12 armoured regiments comprising the Indian Armoured Corps in 1947 were joined by four more regiments in the mid-1950s: 20th Lancers, 61st Cavalry (which maintained its horses while its peers moved from armoured cars to tanks), 62nd Cavalry and 63rd Cavalry.

Designated 31st Indian Armoured Division until September 1945, 1st Armoured Division's headquarters had transferred to Indian control where it was variously named 'Black Elephant', 'Airawat' and 'Fakhr I Hind' ('Pride of India'). 255th Indian Tank Brigade, which was redesignated 1st Armoured Brigade and assigned to 1st Armoured Division in June 1946, also joined the new Indian Army in 1947, as did 2nd Independent Armoured Brigade, which had until December 1945 been designated 252nd Indian Armoured Brigade. Much like its Pakistani peers, Indian Army armour comprised a relatively small number of modern tanks supplemented by older designs that a modern, contemporary army would have since removed from front-line combat operations.

Concerned by China's increasing prominence on the world stage, India garnered military hardware from Britain and, to a lesser degree, France and the United States, although Soviet offers of arms were initially declined to avoid upsetting relations with the West. In 1952, 200 more M4 Shermans were acquired from the United States; these were augmented in 1956 by the arrival of 120 Centurions Mk IIIs from Britain, and then a further 100 Centurion Mk 7s plus 16 Centurion armoured recovery vehicles (ARV) during the following year. In 1957–58, 164 AMX-13 light tanks were acquired from France. However, India was beginning to look to the Soviet Union for its military hardware, which led to the arrival of 178

Indian Army soldiers in the Jammu–Kashmir region during the 1965 war. Both sides were being supplied with a preponderance of British weapons and equipment at this time, as evidenced by the closest fighter who carries a Rifle, Short Magazine, Lee Enfield, Mk III. As a bolt-action, single-shot rifle, the Mk III's magazine held five rounds of .303in ammunition. As with his Pakistani contemporary, the individual Indian soldier was patriotic, and exhibited a similar degree of bravery in combat. Although the Indian Army forces were numerically superior overall, at the opening of hostilities the two sides' forces along the border between Akhnur and Lahore were roughly equal in strength. (Marvin Lichtner/The LIFE Images Collection/Getty Images)

PT-76 amphibious light tanks in 1964–65. Some examples of this Soviet design would see action with 7th Light Cavalry in 1965, but Indian Army commanders were reluctant to use them in combat during the conflict. That year also saw the first deliveries of the T-54 from the Soviet Union; and along with the T-55, Soviet-supplied main battle tanks would equip India's armoured forces in 1971's war with Pakistan. Also starting to appear in 1965 – but not in the front line – was the Vijayanta ('Victorious') main battle tank: based on the British Vickers Mk 1 Main Battle Tank, this was India's first indigenously produced tank, and would make its combat debut in 1971.

PAKISTAN

Pakistan did not inherit any higher organizations for armour, and had to start from scratch when assembling its Armoured Corps after 1947. The Armoured Corps Centre and School was established in November 1947 at Nowshera. In 1950, US-provided tanks and associated vehicles began to arrive to supplement those bequeathed to Pakistan in 1947. Initial US deliveries of 100 Shermans and ten M32 ARVs were followed by 150 M24 Chaffee and 50 M41 Walker Bulldog light tanks in 1954–55 (the M41s would not be fielded in 1965). A total of 347 M47 Patton tanks arrived during 1955–60, with 25 M36 Jackson tank destroyers arriving in 1958.

Pakistan's six armoured regiments were joined by four more in the mid-1950s, namely 4th Cavalry, 12th Cavalry, 15th Lancers and 20th Lancers. As a result of reducing an armoured regiment's tank complement from 75 to a more manageable 44, the excess tanks were used to create four more regiments in 1962 – 22nd, 23rd, 24th and 25th Cavalry – to address what Pakistan considered to be its increasing defence needs. In 1961–64, 200 M48 Patton tanks were delivered by the United States, alongside 109 M113 armoured personnel carriers that were destined for Pakistan's mechanized-infantry regiments.

American efforts to maintain what it considered to be a military balance between India and Pakistan were encouraged by both India and Pakistan in an attempt to further their own political and defence agendas. Realizing that it lacked the manufacturing capability to fight an attritional war with India, Pakistan opted for what it considered to be quality – especially with the M48 Patton. This foreign dependence, however, proved worrisome, for with military hardware from the United States comprising upwards of 80 per cent of such imports, an American reluctance to continue providing support in the years leading up to the 1965 conflict forced Pakistan to look elsewhere to meet its immediate battlefield needs, often to the detriment of logistics and vehicle maintenance.

By September 1965, Pakistan's 23rd Cavalry and 25th Cavalry were incorporated into 10th and 15th Infantry Divisions respectively, with 22nd Cavalry going to 6th Armoured Division, and 24th Cavalry to 1st Armoured Division. In an effort to confuse Indian intelligence, Pakistan also raised what were coined Tank Delivery Units (TDU); four operated during 1965, numbered 30th to 33rd TDU, within 10th, 15th, 11th and 15th Infantry divisions, respectively.

Like the Indian Army, the Pakistan Army would field substantial numbers of Soviet Bloc tanks in the years after 1965, but Pakistan first ordered the T-54, T-55 and PT-76 only in 1968; all three would see combat in Pakistani armoured units during 1971.

To avoid an over-reliance on foreign-produced tanks, starting in 1963 India began producing its own licensed version of the Vickers Mk I Main Battle Tank produced by Vickers-Armstrong. Designed to bestow the capabilities of the upgunned 105mm L7 Centurion, but at a reduced production cost, the Mk I MBT was slated for the export market. Seen here during the 1971 conflict which resulted in Bangladesh's independence, these Indian Army Vijayanta ('Victorious') tanks have a roughly applied, washable paint camouflage. (AFP/Getty Images)

TRAINING, TACTICS AND ORGANIZATION

INDIA

Until the 1965 war, the Indian Army's battlefield experience had comprised relatively minor border fighting and security operations, and not large-scale conventional actions involving integrating various air and ground units with different logistical requirements and capabilities. Notwithstanding the fact that many Indian Army commanders were inexperienced in the art of orchestrating modern warfare, promotions were often unusually fast to accommodate for the Army's increasing manpower and complexity; only after the 1971 Indo-Pakistani War would Indian Army senior commanders perform sufficiently well while in command of formations higher than regimental level. In 1965, unlike the operations of larger formations, squadron- and company-level efforts would be consistently conducted with greater coordination and impact.

Leadership of India's armed forces mostly consisted of the officers recruited on a large scale from the Officers Training Centres established all over the country after the Chinese invasion of 1962, since at that time there happened to be an acute shortage of officers. Almost all training for mid-level Indian Army officers was undertaken at British institutions; starting in the mid-1950s, most senior officers received training in the UK at Sandhurst, Bovington or Wellington. By the 1960s, British military doctrine had matured in addressing the issue of how to maintain effectiveness on a nuclear battlefield. Where the tank had once been the core asset around which to develop doctrine, by the 1960s the potential use of tactical nuclear weapons had supplanted it. At this time British armoured brigades either comprised two armoured regiments and one mechanized-infantry battalion, or one armoured regiment and two mechanized-infantry battalions.

All Indian Armoured Corps officers received extensive instruction at the Armoured Corps Training School in Ahmednagar, while the Armoured Corps Training Centres at Lucknow, Ferozepur and Babina provided for coursework and real-world experience. During their time at these facilities, Indian Army tankers undertook training on

CENTURION TURRET LAYOUT

The Centurion's forward section was divided, with the driver's compartment to the right. Main-gun ammunition was stored to the driver's left, along with an equipment stowage box and drinking-water tank. The driver's split double entry hatch had two rotating No. 15 periscopes. An open area to the fighting compartment's rear held a pair of CO$_2$ fire extinguishers. Two steering levers, one to the left and the other to the right, were anchored to the floor just ahead of the driver's seat, with a gear lever positioned between the two and clutch, brake and accelerator pedals arrayed left to right at his feet.

The central fighting compartment accommodated the commander and gunner on the right, with the commander sitting behind the gunner. The commander's rotatable cupola comprised seven No. 7 Mk 1 episcopes and one No. 8 episcope, each with prismatic Plexiglas vision blocks. Just behind the commander, a container with three haversacks

and three satchels was anchored against the hull rear. A map case, Sten gun, No. 10 wireless station and No. 88 Type A wireless set were nearby, as were water bottles and episcope spares. Positioned in the left of the turret, the loader/radio operator performed his duties opposite the breech, which bisected the turret's interior. The vehicle's C42 wireless set had to be tuned every five minutes and the B47 wireless set calibrated every ten minutes.

An auxiliary engine mounted in the engine compartment's front-left corner drove the generator and ventilating fan. It operated separately from the main engine, and its controls were on the fighting compartment's bulkhead. A starter engine was centrally mounted in the fighting compartment against the engine bulkhead. The transmission, main brakes and final drive assemblies were at the vehicle's far rear.

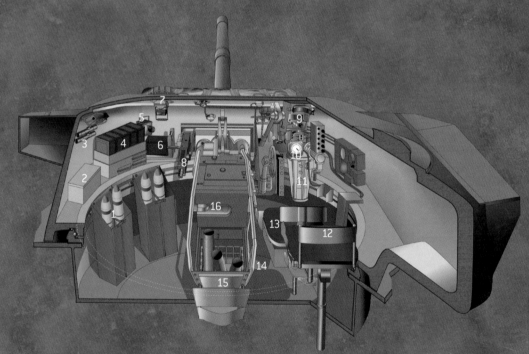

1. HE 20-pdr rounds
2. Spare prisms for loader's periscope
3. Antenna-rod cases
4. .30-calibre MG ammunition boxes
5. Electric hand lamp
6. MG ammunition box in feed tray

7. Loader's No. 15 Mk 1 periscope
8. .30-calibre machine gun
9. Gunner's periscope
10. Compass
11. Turret traverse motor
12. Commander's seat

13. Gunner's seat
14. Breech guard
15. Spent cartridge bin
16. Breech

M48 TURRET LAYOUT

The M48 driver used a steering wheel which, when the cross-drive transmission was placed in the high or low range, allowed the tank to be steered to the left or right. With the transmission in neutral, a full turn of the wheel caused the vehicle to pivot in place, as the tracks moved in opposite directions. The driver's small Reuleaux-shaped hatch pivoted to starboard, and in doing so automatically lowered the three retractable T25 periscopes. The driver's compartment included a pair of fire extinguishers flanking his seat; an accelerator on the floor, with a foot brake higher up on the hull; and an instrument panel to the right, near an engine primer pump, blackout drive switch, and an auxiliary engine choke-throttle control box.

The commander's cupola comprised four M17 vision blocks (periscopes) that provided all-round visibility. The M48 crew lacked the customary fifth member, a radio operator/hull machine-gunner; this meant that the loader was subsequently made responsible for operating the communications equipment, working within an inherited British network enabling communication from regimental to troop level via SCR 528 and No. 19 radio sets. The loader's position on the left of the turret had a hatch in the turret roof, and he typically kept ten ready rounds nearby. On the right of the turret and ahead of the commander, the gunner had a telescopic sight. For crew protection, 180 rounds of .45-calibre SMG M3A1, and 180 rounds of .30-calibre M2 carbine ammunition were carried, in addition to eight hand grenades.

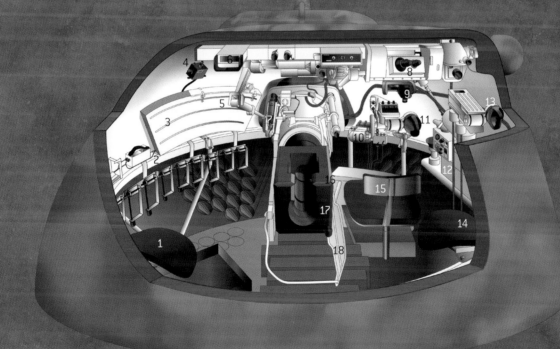

1. Loader's seat
2. Ammunition ready rack
3. .30-caliber ammunition bin
4. Telephone intercom
5. Sight linkage
6. Rangefinder
7. 7.62mm M73 machine gun

8. Optical rangefinder
9. Gunner's periscope
10. Manual elevating pump handle
11. Gunner's control handle
12. Ballistic computer
13. Commander's control handle and
    firing switch

14. Commander's seat
15. Gunner's seat
16. Firing switch
17. Breech
18. Breech guard

Indian soldiers in Jammu and Kashmir manhandle a World War II-vintage, British-provided 25-pdr artillery piece. Although the Indian Army possessed more artillery pieces, its field, medium, heavy and light anti-aircraft regiments were respectively equipped with 25-pdr, 5.5in, 7.2in and 40mm weapons of World War II vintage. The Indian Army lacked medium self-propelled artillery and modern anti-aircraft guns, and its armoured formations correspondingly lacked flexibility and adequate hitting power. In contrast, the Pakistan Army was equipped with some of the latest US weapons, including roughly double the amount of anti-tank assets. Supporting Indian Army infantry were also often all too willing to request artillery assistance when encountering resistance – a problem exacerbated by many units failing to dig protective foxholes or entrenchments during a halt. (Cody Images)

British-supplied Centurions; this included the usual mix of phases, such as 'Driving and Maintenance', which included operating their mounts over a variety of terrain types, as well as track and vehicle repair, and firing exercises. Much of the instruction was inspired by what the Germans had developed during World War II, especially regarding small units, and was derived from British War Office pamphlets such as WO 279/312 'Royal Armoured Corps training technique of shooting from armoured fighting vehicles part 2: application of fire from Centurion tanks', a 1960 publication which provided valuable insight that would be reflected in the level of success Indian Army Centurion crews later achieved against Pakistan Army M48 Pattons.

During the 1965 conflict, Indian Army armour endeavoured to promote speed, flexibility and concentration, but generally operated in a conservative manner. When conducting offensive operations, establishing a firm base from which to attack was deemed paramount in order to offer support during success, or to act as a relatively secure fall-back position. Without such a base, should an attack falter, armour was susceptible to counter-attack that risked its disintegration. When conducting such operations, Indian Army commanders would often resort to unsophisticated frontal assaults, and proved unable or unwilling to adjust flexibly to developing battlefield situations, which caused unnecessary casualties. Commanders were expected to conduct their formations from forward positions to best influence their progress. Unlike those of Pakistan, India's armoured formations relied on an outdated communication system. Jeeps were used extensively for reconnaissance, with AMX-13 light tanks providing heavier support.

In addition to their generally cautious mentality toward offensive operations – somewhat reminiscent of British forces during World War II – Indian senior commanders promoted methodical actions to better maintain control across a chaotic battlefield, and provide sufficient logistics. Fuel was commonly transported in 200-gallon (909-litre) barrels and manhandled onto the tanks' engine decks, and dry rations were the norm. Corps of Electrical and Mechanical Engineers personnel mounted in 1st Armoured Division's Centurion ARVs provided valuable repair capabilities in the field. Medical evacuation remained outdated and inefficient, and helicopters were generally employed in hospital facilities in the rear only.

On paper, each of the Indian Army's armoured regiments had a strength of 45 tanks divided among three squadrons. Each squadron had 14 tanks, subdivided into an HQ (two tanks) and four troops (three tanks each).

PAKISTAN

From 1947 until 1958, the Pakistan Army remained a comparatively small but very competent force, in which most personnel had simple backgrounds, took pride in the profession and were loyal to the Constitutional Government. Once martial law was established in October 1958, the priorities of service personnel to the state changed, as loyalty to Ayub Khan and the ruling regime was subsequently given priority. Within such a system, senior commanders were more often chosen for their political connections and loyalty than their skill and ability; many had served during World War II within a British system that provided good training, although a shortage of officers degraded performance. In contrast, the Pakistan Army's younger soldiers exhibited audacity and initiative, which often limited their advancement due mainly to careerist senior leadership promoting a conservative 'zero error' mind-set, and their often placing personal gain above the good of their commands.

By September 1965, perhaps the Pakistan Army's greatest battlefield weakness was a training system that neglected to provide a thorough training regimen, in which realism would better enable soldiers to acclimate to combat conditions and instil confidence, especially among the considerable influx of new recruits. Administrative staff, planners and instructors all too often possessed minimal skills in developing the framework necessary for regular professional Army officers, with a poorly organized curriculum, and commonly neglected an examination upon completion.

Pakistan Army armoured training focused on the integration of infantry during offensive action, with an emphasis on manoeuvre and outflanking an opponent. During training, British-made Bren Gun Carriers of World War II vintage were commonly used as tank supplements. Later, trainees were taught tank driving (although the Armoured Corps Centre and School at Nowshera lacked an obstacle course), operation and maintenance, as well as using wireless sets and communication, although not in settings that replicated battlefield conditions. A 'Crew Commander's Course' was similar to the basic gunnery course, while a nine-month 'Technical Officers Course' taught tank and vehicle maintenance. A two-week tactics course provided basic battle-drill skills, including a 'Tac-Armour' component that was divided between 'junior tac' for captains and 'senior tac' for majors.

While the M48 Patton's targeting and rangefinding systems were perhaps more complex than those of other tanks of the period, related crew training in the Pakistan Army was poor at best. Those recruits who showed promise or had received a better education tended to be directed to become wireless operators, or tank drivers.

To provide for the training of larger formations, and to give officers potentially valuable experience, several Pakistan Army exercises were conducted between 1947 and 1965, including *Hazard* (1952), *Vulcan* (1953), *November Handicap* (1954),

In concert with advanced Army Navy/Ground Radio Component (AN/GRC) radio equipment, Pakistan Army mechanized infantry were taught to closely follow their accompanying armour into combat, and to provide the 'eyes and ears' for the vehicle, and close support, with additional .50-calibre firepower from their armoured personnel carrier. The AN/GRC series of radios had evolved from World War II-era Signal Corps Radio (SCR) varieties in that they could transmit and receive radio teletype signals on a frequency shift basis. Such VHF systems tended to have greater range, which was less impacted by vegetation and terrain. (Keystone-France/Gamma-Keystone via Getty Images)

ARDESHIR BURZARJI TARAPORE

Lieutenant-Colonel Ardeshir 'Adi' Burzarji Tarapore was born on 18 August 1923 in Bombay, Maharashtra. During World War II he was assigned to 7th Hyderabad Infantry, Hyderabad State Force in 1942, and then to 1st Hyderabad Lancers with whom he saw action in North Africa. Transferred to 17th Horse on 1 April 1951, Tarapore eventually assumed command of the regiment as a lieutenant-colonel, and during the 1965 conflict led it against Phillora during Operation *Riddle*.

Advancing along the right flank of the main offensive south-east of Sialkot, on 11 September 1965, 17th Horse attempted to provide the main attack on Phillora, which developed as a surprise movement into the Pakistani rear between Phillora and Chawinda. During the effort, Pakistani armour counter-attacked from Wazirwali; Tarapore's command countered this effort, and followed up with its own counter-attack using one full Indian tank squadron of 14 Centurion Mk 7s. Though wounded in the arm during the fighting, Tarapore refused to be evacuated.

On 14 September, Tarapore led his regiment to capture Wazirwali, and two days later, Jassoran and Butur-Dograndi. During this battle his tank, 'Khushab' (named for the 1856 British battlefield victory during the Anglo-Persian War), was hit several times, but the unit remained unmoved, and managed to assist supporting Indian Army infantry reportedly to knock out 60 Pakistani tanks, suffering only nine tank casualties in the process. During the engagement, Tarapore was standing in his cupola when a Pakistani round struck his mount, killing him and setting the vehicle on fire. Personnel of the Pakistan Army's 25th Cavalry subsequently took the Centurion as a trophy. Cremated on the battlefield, Tarapore was posthumously awarded India's highest wartime gallantry medal, the *Param Vir Chakra* ('Wheel (or Cross) of the Ultimate Brave').

Established on 26 January 1967, the 36mm-diameter *Raksha* ('Defence') Medal was awarded for Indian service in the 1965 Indo-Pakistani War. Made of copper-nickel, the obverse showed the national emblem of the Ashokan Lions above the Indian National motto, 'Truth Alone Prevails'. The award's reverse comprised a rising sun over crossed laurels, with the top reading '*Raksha* Medal' in Hindi, with '1965'. (Public Domain)

Agility (1956), *Tezgam* (1960) and *Milestone* (1961). Starting in the early 1960s, many Pakistani officers received additional training in the United States, at the US Army Armor School at Fort Knox, Kentucky, and the Infantry School at Fort Benning, Georgia. Such experience was of limited value, however, considering the lavish provision of *matériel* in the American military, in sharp contrast to the realities of fighting in Jammu and Kashmir.

As a main battle tank the M48 Patton could be used in a variety of combat roles, including delaying, attack and exploitation, with emphasis on movement, to the near exclusion of incorporating a fire component. In the defensive role, the M48 was to be allocated to supporting built-up positions or as dug-in artillery. Although Pakistani armour, such as the M48, possessed an ability to operate at night thanks to the use of infrared equipment, the accuracy of night-time firing was considerably reduced compared to that of daytime firing. Several key factors regarding any successful tank operation included effective reconnaissance and the use of terrain, such as avoiding moving across the crest of a hill and thus unnecessarily exposing the vehicle's

GHULAM MEHDI KHAN SHAHEED

Acting Lance Dafadar Ghulam Mehdi Khan Shaheed grew up on a farm, alongside his three older siblings, and volunteered with the Pakistan Army. As an athlete who excelled at basketball, and a patriot, with war starting he was excited to be summoned to his local unit, 11th Cavalry.

Having moved forward from Kotla the night before, at the start of Operation *Grand Slam* on 1 September 1965 the regiment (minus A Squadron) was part of 102nd Infantry Brigade, which anchored the right flank of 12th Infantry Division's lengthy frontage, and was to maintain contact with the adjacent 7th Infantry Division to its south. During the brigade's advance to the Munawwarwali Tawi River, M48 Pattons from B Squadron, 11th Cavalry moved against the town of Chumb and the defending Indian Army AMX-13s of C Squadron, 20th Lancers. From the south, C Squadron's M36B2 Jackson tank destroyers provided assistance, as Pakistani forces sought to achieve a crossing over the waterway.

During the attack, Mehdi Khan was patrolling in his M48 when a recoilless-rifle round struck the vehicle's track, immobilizing it. With the likelihood of another projectile finishing the job, the crew baled out and sought cover from Indian small-arms crossfire. With one of the crewmen having been hit, and as per Pakistan Army tradition never to leave a wounded comrade behind, Mehdi Khan returned under fire to carry the crewman to a relatively safe location with his platoon. Although successful, Mehdi Khan was shot and killed. Due to his act of valour, determination and commitment towards his objective, Mehdi Khan was awarded the *Tamgha-e-Jurat* ('Medal of Courage').

The 35mm-diameter bronze *Sitara-i-Harb 1385* ('Indo-Pakistani War 1965') was awarded to Pakistani personnel for combat service during the conflict. Its obverse displayed the *Shahadat* ('There is no God but God and Muhammad is His Messenger') surrounded by the medal's name, *Istar-i-Herb*, in Urdu and Bengali. Its obverse had a circle, which often surrounded the medal's name. (Public Domain)

silhouette. According to doctrine, the employment of mass and mobility was to be used to strike an important or weak enemy sector with maximum violence, and to overwhelm and exploit it by penetrating into the enemy's command, control and communications zone. As casualties were directly proportional to the time needed to close with an objective, initiative and aggression were paramount, but often lacking when under fire.

Although derived from a British military framework, the Pakistani military also drew inspiration from the American emphasis on massive fire support in concert with armour, and a defensive concept of a semi-mobile defensive system. Such doctrine promoted a battle zone comprised of a series of control points, with support from nearby quick-reaction forces. Counter-attacks were to be launched by armour and infantry groups, supported by frequently heavy and sustained artillery fire using variable time fuses to maximize destruction and degrade the enemy's resolve, as rounds fired at different trajectories would arrive on target in greater numbers than if fired with identical settings. The Chinese penchant for multi-directional attacks was

Pakistani M47 Pattons abandoned in the Asal Uttar sector. The vehicle at right sports the number '34' in red with white outlines. Note the soft terrain, as evidenced by the deep track trails, and that the .50-calibre Browning machine guns are absent from their turret pintle mounts. (bharat-rakshak.com)

similarly emulated, and included intensive digging and tunnelling in villages, and employing paramilitary forces for infiltration. Unlike India, Pakistan tended to maintain strong mobile reserves comprised of armour, reconnaissance and mechanized infantry to support a minimally manned front line, and then reinforce as necessary.

On paper, each Pakistan Army armoured regiment fielded 44 tanks divided among three squadrons – a figure that had been reduced from an unwieldy 75 after 1960, and which allowed for forming 22nd, 23rd, 24th and 25th Cavalry in 1962. Each armoured regiment included a Headquarters and Headquarters Troop, and three armoured squadrons, each with a Headquarters and Headquarters Troop, three Armoured Troops, a Tank Company, and a Field Artillery Battery.

ARMOURED STRENGTH IN 1965

INDIA

On 1 September 1965 the Indian Army fielded 584 tanks including 186 Centurions, 308 Shermans and 90 AMX-13s. (The M5 Stuarts had been withdrawn in early 1965, and did not participate in the war. Forty-five or so PT-76s would be fielded by 7th Light Cavalry later in September.) These tanks served in 16 armoured regiments, of which 14 would be employed in combat during the conflict.

To concentrate the best available tanks into a single formation, the Indian Army's Centurion Mk 7s were incorporated into 1st Armoured Division, which was subordinated to Lieutenant-General P.O. Dunn's recently formed I Corps, itself a part of Lieutenant-General Harbakhsh Singh's Western Command. On the verge of retirement in September 1965, Major-General Rajinder 'Sparrow' Singh commanded 1st Armoured Division based near Jalandhar, about 80km south-east of Amritsar. On 1 September, 1st Armoured Division's armoured elements included 4th Horse, 16th Light Cavalry and 17th Horse, organized into Brigadier K.K. Singh's 1st Armoured

Although it was nearing the end of its front-line life as a medium tank by 1945, two decades later the M4 Sherman filled out several Indian Army armoured regiments in the form of British-provided M4A1(76)s and M4A4(76)s, and Pakistan Army armoured regiments in the form of American-provided M4A3E4s and M4A1E4s. The M4A3 shown here in Indian service in 1966 retains a 75mm main gun. The three vertical pieces on the turret side held extra track lengths, and served as an additional degree of armoured protection. To avoid exposing internally housed rounds in the turret, they were stored in the hull; those in the forward hull racks received an external 1in (25.4mm) armoured plate welded over the area. Until later 'wet' housings were introduced, such strategically placed add-on armour helped keep the vehicle from living up to its dubious 'Tommy Cooker' moniker due to the apparent ease with which M4s 'brewed up' as a consequence of external projectile impacts triggering internal ammunition explosions. (Cody Images)

Brigade, together with the motorized infantrymen of 9th Dogra. Brigadier H.S. Dhillon's 43rd Lorried Infantry Brigade provided three battalions of motorized infantry in 4-ton lorries, namely 5/9th Gorkha Rifles, 5th Jat and 8th Garhwal Rifles. The division also included the Sherman-equipped 2nd Lancers and 62nd Cavalry; artillery comprised 1st Self-Propelled Artillery, 1st Towed Field Artillery, 1st Medium Field Artillery, and 1st Light Anti-Aircraft regiments. While some of the division's armoured elements were dispersed, the Centurion Mk 7s were concentrated in 4th Horse, 16th Light Cavalry and 17th Horse to provide a sufficient 'punch' when needed.

Also part of the Indian Army's Western Command, Lieutenant-General K.S. Katoch's XV Corps controlled Brigadier T.K. Theogaraj's 2nd (Independent) Armoured Brigade, a corps reserve located at Patiala/Nabha-Sangrur and fielding Lieutenant-Colonel Salim Caleb's 3rd Cavalry (the Indian Army's fourth Centurion-equipped regiment) and the AMX-13-equipped 8th Light Cavalry. Additional Indian Army armoured units that saw combat in 1965 included 1st Horse, 14th Horse, 18th Cavalry, The Central India Horse (unofficially called 21st Horse) and The Deccan Horse (unofficially called 9th Horse) – all of which were equipped with Shermans – as well as 7th Light Cavalry (PT-76) and 20th Lancers (AMX-13).

PAKISTAN

On 1 September 1965 the Pakistan Armoured Corps fielded 886 tanks and tank destroyers including 230 M47 Pattons, 202 M48 Pattons, 308 M4A1E4 and M4A3E4 Shermans and 96 M24 Chaffees, within 18 armoured regiments; two regiments, 11th Cavalry and 25th Cavalry, operated a total of 50 M36B1 tank destroyers. In all, 17 of Pakistan's 18 armoured regiments saw combat in the conflict.

The Pakistan Army fielded two armoured divisions during the conflict: 1st Armoured Division and the still forming 6th Armoured Division. At full strength, each division was to comprise two armoured brigades that were configured as 'combat commands' when operational, plus supporting artillery, engineers and other units. Each armoured brigade was meant to contain three armoured regiments, as well as a

Indian soldiers examine a Pakistani M24 Chaffee light tank, examples of which were still in front-line service as late as 1971. The '20' in the yellow circle indicates the vehicle's approximate weight for gauging bridge strength. The white horizontal turret stripe served for Identification Friend or Foe purposes. (Cody Images)

Reconnaissance Troop, with six 106mm recoilless guns, and a mechanized-infantry battalion that would be transported into battle in tracked, amphibious M113 armoured personnel carriers.

On 1 September 1965, Major-General Nasir Ahmad Khan's 1st Armoured Division comprised two armoured brigades. Brigadier Anthony Lumb's 4th Armoured Brigade included 4th Cavalry and 5th Horse, with its mechanized-infantry component being 10th Frontier Force. Brigadier Bashir's 5th Armoured Brigade fielded 6th Lancers, 24th Cavalry and the motorized infantry of 1st Frontier Force. Divisional artillery support was provided by 3rd, 15th and 16th Field regiments (105mm), as well as 21st Medium Regiment (155mm), while 12th Cavalry provided divisional reconnaissance. 19th (Self Propelled) Light Anti-Aircraft Regiment and 1st Engineer Battalion provided additional support.

When it entered combat, Major-General Abrar Hussain's 6th Armoured Division – still forming in 1965 – included The Guides Cavalry (unofficially called 10th Cavalry), 11th Cavalry and 22nd Cavalry, all equipped with the M48 Patton. The division's additional units included the motorized infantry of 9th Frontier Force and also 1st (Self-Propelled) Artillery Regiment. Significantly, brigade-level commands were not formed for 6th Armoured Division, hampering command and control.

Pakistani M47s that have been abandoned in a wheat field near Mahmudpura, in the Khem Karan sector. The farmers await the arrival of Indian Army Corps of Electrical and Mechanical Engineers personnel to remove the vehicles; the nearest of which, '34', looks to have suffered damage to its breech mechanism. (bharat-rakshak.com)

Although not allocated to combat in 1965, Brigadier Moin-ud-Din's 3rd Armoured Brigade comprised 19th Lancers and the motorized infantry of 7th Frontier Force – the only such battalion to operate the M113 APC at the time of the conflict. Parcelled out to non-armoured formations, the remainder of the Pakistan Army's armoured regiments included 13th Lancers, 15th Lancers, 20th Lancers, 23rd Cavalry, 25th Cavalry, 30th TDU, 31st TDU, 32nd TDU and 33rd TDU.

THE STRATEGIC SITUATION

THE ROAD TO WAR

The post-war political and financial cost of retaining an increasingly fractured India forced Britain – virtually bankrupt at World War II's conclusion in 1945 – to agree to withdraw from the region, and grant it independence. With a partitioning of the Subcontinent scheduled for 1947, its numerous princely states were officially to join the Domains or Hindu India, or the largely Muslim regions to its north-east and north-west, respectively named East and West Pakistan. Amid widespread rioting and retribution that claimed some 500,000 lives, nearly 15 million people were displaced in what was recorded as history's largest mass migration.

Following the creation of the Dominion of Pakistan on 15 August 1947, Muhammad Ali Jinnah (1876–1948), its first Governor-General, stressed that Islamic idealism remained incomplete as long as the majority Muslim Jammu and Kashmir remained separate from Pakistan, even though the coveted region struggled to maintain its own independence, and resisted pressure to join either political entity. To settle the matter in Pakistan's favour, on 3 September, Muslim tribal militias from the North-West Frontier Province were sent into Jammu and Kashmir to foment unrest, as a prelude to allocating official military personnel to restore order. In response, the princely state's Hindu ruler requested and received assistance from India, at the cost of being

A late-production M5A1 Stuart light tank of the Indian Army patrolling a New Delhi street during a lull in rioting. Although the M5A1 – a roomier version of the M5 – was effective in providing infantry support during constricted jungle fighting, or reconnaissance in World War II, by the conflict's end the M24 Chaffee was replacing it in service. The M5A1's 37mm M6 main gun and thin armour precluded it from operating beyond police or security duties, and by 1965 both India and Pakistan had removed their Stuarts from front-line service. The horizontal plates across the glacis helped deflect shrapnel and debris from exposed crewmen; and in addition to a bow-mounted M1919A4 .30-calibre machine gun, the vehicle incorporated one coaxially to the main gun, and another attached to the turret roof for anti-aircraft or local defence. Having a more powerful radio than preceding Stuarts, the M5A1's turret bustle (barely visible) housed an SCR 508, while the small nub atop the turret accommodated a searchlight. Note the fire extinguisher on the hull roof and the tow cable. (Keystone/Getty Images)

incorporated into India's domain. Although Indian air and ground forces subsequently entered the conflict zone and ejected the Muslim militias, fighting officially continued until the United Nations mandated a ceasefire in 1949, which through a mutual signing of the Karachi Agreement (27 July 1949) established a border along Jammu and Kashmir – although by now cross-border skirmishes and minor incursions were the norm.

In an effort to bolster its cause – and thereby gain military support, especially American – Pakistan joined the South-East Asia Treaty Organization (in 1954) and the Central Treaty Organization (in 1955), which worked to counter the spread of Communism. As part of the US effort to counter Communist expansion into southern Asia, starting in the late 1950s large amounts of American military and financial aid poured into Pakistan, providing armour, artillery, aircraft and other *matériel* – much of it superior to the Indian equivalents. After 11 years of a fledgling parliamentary democracy, in 1958 the armed forces took control of running Pakistan's administration, which created a degree of stability and economic growth; the transition was to the country's detriment, however, as such a centralized, authoritarian framework stifled progressive institutions, and maintained a militarized status quo.

Seeking to transform Pakistan's military into a modern fighting force, the United States agreed to upgrade five-and-a-half divisions with contemporary weapons, and provide some $100 million between 1954 and 1962. By 1965, Pakistan's military expenditure amounted to 6 per cent of GNP (compared to India's 3.7 per cent). Commensurate with these expenditures, the Pakistan Army expanded from 160,000 personnel in 1961 to some 250,000 by 1965, with roughly 1 per cent of males between the ages of 15 and 64 serving; this figure was bolstered by 30,000 lightly armed 'Azad Kashmir' militia. On 8 September 1965, after the outbreak of war with India, the United States decided to place an arms embargo on both belligerent nations; and with limited domestic industry, Pakistan had most to lose from this decision.

While many Indian politicians advocated that the country should avoid becoming entangled in 'great power' matters, the Subcontinent's geographic and political importance all but ensured India's involvement in international affairs. Although non-aligned, India viewed China's invasion and occupation of an independent Tibet in 1950–51 as a threat to its own northern border and security. With its military having performed poorly during China's invasion of northern Jammu and Kashmir in October–November 1962 – and also while skirmishing with Pakistan over the Rann of Kutch, an area of salt marshes – India embarked on a programme to address its apparent military shortcomings. From December 1962 to February 1963, several conferences were held between India and Pakistan concerning Kashmir; although these offered a chance to solve outstanding differences equitably, after the Sino-Indian War, on 2 March 1963 Pakistan signed a bilateral border agreement with its new Chinese ally, and relations with India soured. The expansion of the Indian armed forces – from 550,000 personnel before 1962 to 870,000 by 1965 – was viewed by most Pakistanis as being directed towards them rather than China. By 1964 the Soviets

had become India's primary arms supplier, but India's path to military modernization continued to suffer from poor planning, doctrine that largely neglected inter-service coordination, and a mismatching of technologies with strategy.

Although asymmetric actions – such as the mysterious disappearance of a holy relic believed to be the Prophet Muhammad's hair from the Hazratbal Shrine in Srinagar on 26 December 1963 – had triggered rioting and suspicion among the region's Muslim population, Pakistan struggled to instigate a 'People's War' in the Kashmir Valley. In June 1965, as part of an intensification of its aggressive activities along the Jammu and Kashmir boundary, Pakistan reportedly forced employers to release all military reservists, which provided for an irregular 'Mujahid' force under Pakistan Army control. As a diversion to its primary goal in the north, Pakistan inserted conventional forces into the disputed Rann of Kutch; although a largely desolate region, the Rann of Kutch's proximity to Karachi, the capital of Pakistan, seemed to the Pakistanis to make it a possible battle zone. With India regarded as unwilling or unable to prosecute a war effectively, in August 1965 President Muhammad Ayub Khan (1907–74) confidently launched Operation *Gibraltar*, in which thousands of motivated, well-armed Islamic paramilitary personnel infiltrated Indian-administered Jammu and Kashmir to sabotage military installations, disrupt communications and promote social discord. Although results of the operation were mixed as Indian forces soon expelled many of these groups, it portended the conventional war Pakistan hoped to avoid.

OPERATION *GRAND SLAM*

By 1965, senior Pakistani commanders had approved plans to sever the Jammu–Srinagar road, thereby denying India ground access to Jammu and Kashmir. Major-General Akhtar Hussain Malik, General Officer Commanding (GOC) 12th Infantry Division, subsequently developed a four-step plan to secure the targeted area before India could effectively react. The Pakistanis envisaged an attack in which 12th Infantry Division – supported by two Patton-equipped armoured regiments, namely 11th Cavalry and 13th Lancers, plus a company of infantry from 9th Frontier Force and a detachment of 15th Military Police Unit – would quickly capture Akhnur, nearly 40km from the Cease-Fire Line. In what were intended as consecutive actions, 102nd Infantry Brigade, with armour support, was to advance to the Munawwarwali Tawi River, some 7km east of the Cease-Fire Line; 10th Infantry Brigade would then cross the waterway and make for Akhnur. Once these objectives were achieved, Malik – designated Operation *Grand Slam*'s overall commander – was to direct additional forces toward Rauauri and the town of Jammu. Once these Pakistani moves had been accomplished, India would likely have to employ much of Lieutenant-General P.O. Dunn's I Corps in attempting to recapture the key location at the expense of other sectors. Commensurately, a thrust mounted further south, in the area between the Ravi and Sutlej rivers, by Pakistan's 1st Armoured Division was expected to contain and destroy at least three Indian infantry divisions in the Beas–Ravi Corridor, while Pakistan's still-forming 6th Armoured Division along its right (north) was well positioned to deal with any Indian armoured counter-thrust launched between the Ravi and Chenab rivers.

Following a three-hour preparatory bombardment, Pakistani ground forces launched their attack at 0500hrs on 1 September. Once the town of Chumb was secured, the route towards the vital Akhnur Bridge over the Chenab River would essentially be open – but the bridge lacked the strength to permit heavy armoured traffic. Despite their disarray, however, the defending Indian infantry forces, supported by artillery and small numbers of AMX-13 light tanks and recoilless guns, would retard Pakistani progress towards Akhnur. With its tanks under-utilized and poorly employed, the Pakistan Army's 6:1 armour advantage was largely negated by parcelling out 11th Cavalry and 13th Lancers' tanks instead of keeping them concentrated. In response to the deteriorating situation in the Chumb sector, at 1645hrs on 1 September the Indian Minister of Defence, Y.B. Chavan, decisively authorized air support, knowing it could escalate the conflict. The Pakistani advance steadily drove a wedge between Mandiala and Chumb, and by 1830hrs, the Pakistan Army's 13th Lancers reached the Munawwarwali Tawi River. With the defence along the border now untenable, a general Indian withdrawal took place. At 2200hrs, ten Pakistani Patton tanks crossed to the Munawwarwali Tawi River's eastern bank.

As the Pakistani offensive continued its eastward advance during the morning of 2 September, seemingly destined to achieve its operational goals, President Ayub Khan notified Major-General Malik that Major-General Muhammad Yahya Khan, GOC 7th Infantry Division, was to take control of *Grand Slam*. Although the Pakistanis had essentially cleared the area up to the Munawwarwali Tawi River, instead of forging ahead against a still disorganized enemy, Yahya Khan opted to halt to organize and resupply his own forces, stating his concern about what was an imagined Indian Army build-up. Instead of aiding the Pakistanis, the command change gave the Indians a day's respite in which to strengthen their defences. In a surprisingly leisurely manner, at 1430hrs Yahya Khan issued orders for crossing the Munawwarwali Tawi River, which was largely devoid of Indian personnel. Throughout the day the AMX-13s of C Squadron, 20th Lancers remained the only Indian Army tank force between the Munawwarwali Tawi River and Akhnur, although the squadron now fielded just three operational vehicles.

During 3–5 September, as the Indian Army's XV Corps frantically tried to stabilize its front, Pakistani forces made slow progress over the broken terrain, interspersed by several watercourses, along the Chenab River to a position from which they could outflank the Indians from the south and pin them against the nearby mountains. With Pakistani armour remaining dispersed, the attackers' artillery was correspondingly hard pressed to provide support; this, in turn, allowed the Indian defenders to engage the enemy tanks piecemeal. By the evening of 5 September, leading elements of Pakistan's 13th Lancers had engaged Indian positions on the Fatwal Ridge. Although Pakistani spearheads had only advanced some 30km in four days, they had reached Jourian, and were now within a few hours' march of Akhnur.

On 4 September, as part of India's planned counter-attack, Lieutenant-General Dunn's I Corps headquarters was established at Kaluchak, near Jammu, while its spearhead, Major-General S.K. Korla's 6th Mountain Division, prepared to attack with Major-General R.K. Ranjit Singh's 14th Infantry Division and Major-General M.L. Thapan's 26th Infantry Division on its left and right, respectively. Tasked with securing the area around Pagowal, Phillora, Chawinda and Badiana, I Corps was to focus on advancing toward the Marala–Ravi Link Canal, and eventually to the Dhallewali–Wuhilam–Daska–Mandhali line. Although India's Operation *Riddle* counter-attack called for a simultaneous attack by I Corps and Lieutenant-General J.S. Dhillon's XI Corps, as the former was still forming at its assembly positions and in the interest of time, Minister of Defence Chavan – with Prime Minister Lal Bahadur Shastri's approval – authorized XI Corps to begin the offensive as soon as possible and take the fight into Pakistan.

Delhi, September 1966: a year after the conflict, Pakistan's Major-General Muhammad Yahya Khan is pictured with one of his Indian opposite numbers. Although Operation *Grand Slam* was well planned, neither Pakistan's president, Ayub Khan, nor her commander-in-chief, General Muhammad Musa Khan, possessed the resolution to fight a decisive war and the skills and insight necessary to achieve a battlefield victory in the Chumb–Jaurian battle. As both men's command styles were also very defensive-minded and reactionary, the longer the fighting continued, the weaker Pakistan's strength became due to mounting casualties; also, its assaulting forces were steadily funnelled into an increasingly constrained battlespace bordered by mountains and the Chenab River, thus reducing the possibility of manoeuvre. (Cody Images)

OPERATION *RIDDLE*

Operation *Riddle* had been secretly formulated during India's mobilization following the recent Rann of Kutch skirmish, for when just such an eventually presented itself. While India had so far remained on the defensive along the Pakistani border, on 1 September, Indian Army HQ issued the code word 'Bangle' to indicate imminent hostilities. The undertaking risked expanding the conflict beyond desirable limits – and, by crossing an international border, political recriminations – and senior Indian

WEST PAK – J&K

India's Chief of Air Staff, Air Marshal Arjan Singh (left), confers with General J.N. Chaudhuri, Chief of the Army Staff in New Delhi on 23 September 1965. After five days of fighting, India's military strength was growing as reinforcements finally arrived in-theatre to provide sufficient forces for a counter-attack. Pakistan's self-defeating effort to capture Akhnur had resulted in a menacing build-up of Indian ground forces; instead of having to focus on recapturing the vital transportation hub connecting it with Jammu and Kashmir, these forces could now concentrate further south. By crossing the Pakistani border to strike for Sialkot – and the country's second-largest city, Lahore, the capital of United Punjab – Indian forces endeavoured to bring the fight into Pakistani territory, and siphon enemy formations from the threatened Akhnur area. (Keystone/Getty Images)

commanders expressed some reservations, among them General J.N. Chaudhuri, Chief of the Army Staff, and Lieutenant-General Harbakhsh Singh, GOC-in-C Western Command. As if to alleviate such concerns about advancing into Pakistani territory near Lahore, Prime Minister Shastri countered that 'The other is also an international border' – in reference to that of Kashmir – and that Indian forces were to 'Cross it'.

According to the Indian Army's Operation Instruction No. 36 (9 August 1965), Western Command was to move forces to their jump-off positions just before attacking, and simultaneously secure the BRB Canal from the Grand Trunk Road to Bedian and a bridgehead over the Ravi River, capture Tanda, and conduct a limited push on Sialkot. Once these objectives were achieved, Indian ground forces were to establish a frontage connecting Dhallewali, Wuhilam-Daska and Mandhali, and advance on Lahore. Lieutenant-General Dhillon's XI Corps and Lieutenant-General Dunn's I Corps were in position to assault Lahore and Sialkot, respectively. This would effectively separate the two defensive regions, and enable India to focus on destroying Pakistan's war potential, but not the cities. The Indians were intent on tying up Pakistani opposition, and reduce the likelihood of a counter-attack as Indian forces were still assembling and organizing. The Ravi River physically separated XI Corps and I Corps; this would impede effective control and coordination, and force the two Indian Army corps to set off at different times.

XI Corps was to move against an 80km stretch of the Pakistani border between the Ravi River and Khem Karan. Using its adequately trained 15th and 7th Infantry divisions and 4th Mountain Division, with support from Brigadier T.K. Theogaraj's 2nd (Independent) Armoured Brigade, Lieutenant-General Dhillon's corps possessed an unusually large complement of infantry and artillery. Unsuited to fighting in largely open terrain where heavier weapons were needed, such mountain formations were needed to strengthen the Indian offensive, even though they were at a disadvantage when compared to fellow infantry formations.

In opposition, five Pakistan Army battalions stretched out over a lengthy front in anticipation of providing a defence. While Operation *Grand Slam* was unfolding to the north, Pakistan had positioned forces along the BRB Canal and Upper Bari Doab Canal to cover the most direct route to Lahore, block the bridge at Dera Baba Nanak, and undertake an offensive in the Khem Karan sector to the south. General Musa believed that India would focus primarily on recapturing lost territory in Jammu and Kashmir, and that if the Indians were to escalate the fighting they would do so along the corridor between the Ravi and Chenab rivers leading to Sialkot, and further south where the Grand Trunk Road connected Wazirabad and Gujranwala. As such, much of the Pakistan Army's 1st Armoured and 7th Infantry divisions had been moved to near Sheikhupura, 30km north-west of Lahore, while 6th Armoured Division assembled near Shakargarh in the Sialkot sector. The Pakistanis also expected the Indians to conduct diversionary actions in Sindh. By keeping Indian forces occupied in the west, the Pakistanis hoped to keep them from attacking East Pakistan.

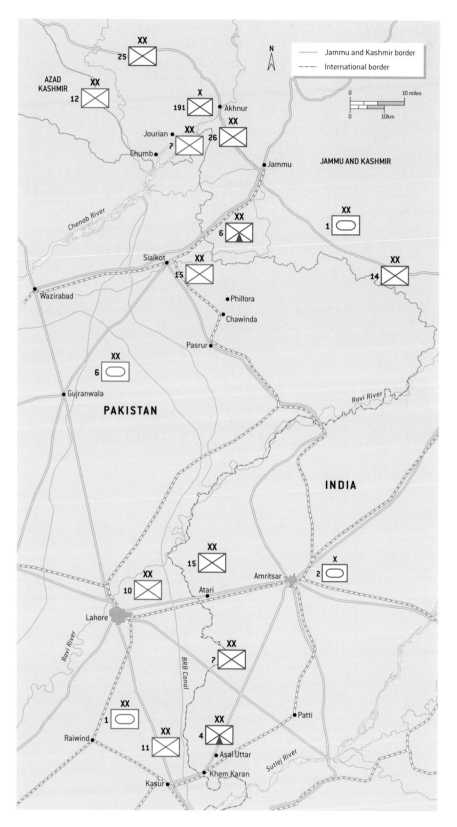

The situation at 0000hrs, 6 September 1965. During the brief 1965 Indo-Pakistani War fighting raged along a roughly 200km front between southern Jammu and Kashmir to around the Sutlej River. Lieutenant-General Bakhtir Rana's I Corps would control all Pakistani ground forces north of Lahore, although these were broken up into corps-level task forces. In practice, the Pakistan Army would field seven divisions (including one armoured, and one forming) along the Indian border, and one in East Pakistan. The Indian Army fielded nine infantry and mountain divisions (of which four were understrength and two deployed further to the north), one independent infantry brigade, one armoured division and one independent armoured brigade.

COMBAT

THE LAHORE FRONT: ASAL UTTAR

OPERATION *RIDDLE* BEGINS

At 0400hrs on 6 September, XI Corps' counter-attack began, making good progress towards Lahore and points south during the early morning. Although minimal Pakistani resistance suggested a relatively easy Indian victory south-east of Lahore, the Pakistanis had built up forces in the area in anticipation of the Indian Army's attack towards Khem Karan; this meant Pakistani resistance steadily increased, and – supported by the Pakistan Air Force and heavy Pakistan Army artillery fire – the defenders pushed the Indians from their early gains along the BRB Canal. Indian Army attacks continued into the night of 6/7 September, particularly on Bedian, Punwan and Pallanwala, but proved unable to penetrate the Pakistani defences.

To conduct limited Pakistani counter-attacks in the sector, Major-General Abdul Hamid Khan's 11th Infantry Division had been given Brigadier Bashir's 5th Armoured Brigade, but so far neither Major-General Nasir Ahmad Khan's 1st Armoured Division nor I Corps' other infantry formations had been committed. On 4 September, papers captured from an Indian Army dispatch rider had confirmed the presence of India's 1st Armoured Division near Samba, and Pakistan's High Command consequently wished to avoid tying up its armour in the rather poor tank terrain north-east of Khem Karan. The desire of Pakistan's senior commanders to strike into East Punjab through this axis remained strong, however.

A North American F-86F Sabre in Pakistan Air Force service. Although the Pakistan Air Force was numerically smaller than that of its adversary, it possessed more modern US-built, NATO-standard aircraft and air bases linked by microwave communication networks, with early-warning radar sets spread along the international border at Peshawar, Multan, Sargodha and Badin. (Cody Images)

PAKISTAN STRIKES

On 7 September, 5th Armoured Brigade moved towards Khem Karan as part of Pakistan's planned offensive. By evening the Pakistani forces had reached Khem Karan and established a bridgehead. Having been checked along the BRB Canal, India's 4th Mountain Division had hastily occupied a defended sector at Asal Uttar ('Fitting Response'), and laid anti-tank mines along the main approaches from the west. The gap to the south-east of Valtoha was flooded by a nearby canal, which presented a formidable defence.

Brigadier Sahib Dad's 21st Infantry Brigade and Brigadier Bashir's 5th Armoured Brigade moved into the bridgehead; Brigadier Anthony Lumb's 4th Armoured Brigade was also to move into the area, as soon as mopping-up operations in Khem Karan had been completed. With the Patton tanks of Lieutenant-Colonel Shahabad Gul's 6th Lancers plus 5th Frontier Force on one axis and 1st Frontier Force (minus one company) plus an M24 Chaffee squadron from 15th Lancers on a second, the Pakistan Army mounted a well-coordinated attack that threw the Indians back. Major-General Abdul Hamid Khan, GOC 11th Infantry Division, who made full use of his helicopters, was able to visit the sector in which the fighting was severest, and could respond quickly to changing battlefield situations. Once thrown back the Indians were unable to reassemble and reorganize, although the tall sugar-cane and cotton crops gave them a degree of cover from their Pakistani pursuers.

During the morning, Pakistani Chaffee and Patton tanks conducted reconnaissance in force, but were rebuffed by Indian Shermans. Pakistan's 4th Armoured Brigade then mounted a frontal assault on 4th Mountain Division in a bid to sever the Khem Karan–Bhikhiwind road in the Cheema area, just north of Asal Uttar. At 1430hrs the Pakistani attack began as three columns moved off; these were comprised of M48 Pattons of 24th Cavalry, M24 Chaffees of B Squadron, 15th Lancers, and 1st Frontier Force, a mechanized-infantry battalion in armoured personnel carriers. At 1445hrs 24th Cavalry conducted a reconnaissance-in-force, during which the Pakistani tanks overran part of the positions held by 1/9th Gorkha Rifles. Acting as a diversion, several Pattons of B Squadron, 24th Cavalry engaged 4th Grenadiers and the gun area, but the Pakistanis were halted near Rattoke.

Next, the Pakistanis tried to bypass the defended area to the north, but Indian Army Centurion Mk 7s of B Squadron, 3rd Cavalry had anticipated the move and

55

A knocked-out and abandoned Pakistani M48 Patton marked '34' near Khem Karan. Its .50-calibre cupola machine gun has been removed. (bharat-rakshak.com)

OPPOSITE With Indian forces having crossed the border the previous day, on 8 September Pakistan launched an attack from south of Lahore, with the intent of pushing to the north-east to strike I Corps' left (southern) flank, and secure crossings over the nearby Beas River. Against the M47 and M48 tanks of Pakistan's 1st Armoured and 11th Infantry divisions, the defending 4th Mountain Division withdrew to establish a horseshoe position into which enemy armour could be baited. Confident of their mounts and optimistic of inflicting an operational defeat, Pakistani tank crews entered the soft terrain of the killing zone in which Indian recoilless rifles and Centurions from 2nd Armoured Brigade took a heavy toll. Combined with the Sialkot sector fighting to the north, the participation of hundreds of armoured vehicles represented the largest such engagement between World War II and the 1973 Sinai battle.

prepared to receive them near Bhikhiwind. The Indian tanks reacted quickly to the emerging threat, and according to Indian sources knocked out five Pattons and a Chaffee, causing the Pakistani force to withdraw. Such Pakistani probing indicated to Indian commanders that a major armoured thrust was to be expected, possibly as early as the next day. The Indian Army's 2nd Independent Armoured Brigade was immediately placed in support near Amritsar, and moved from its assembly area where it was ordered to reposition 3rd Cavalry, minus A Squadron, from the Chabal Kalan area and Rajatal to 4th Mountain Division's sector, and 8th Light Cavalry, less a squadron, from the Amritsar bypass area to 4th Mountain Division's control. During the night of 8/9 September, all moves were effected without incident, and the Indian defences were reinforced with additional mines.

By 1700hrs on 8 September, Pakistan's 6th Lancers had captured Valtoha railway station, some 19km from Khem Karan; but the tanks' advance had outstripped that of the accompanying Pakistan Army infantry, which was involved in clearing small pockets of resistance, snipers and machine-gun nests hidden in crops, and could not keep pace. All along the route, Indian Army rear-echelon units had been taken by surprise. In the centre, 24th Cavalry's advance had also been successful, though not to the same extent as 6th Lancers' right hook. Under Lieutenant-Colonel Ali Imam, 24th Cavalry had crossed the line of Asal Uttar some 13km from Khem Karan. However, Brigadier Bashir appears to have made a mistake in gauging the extent to which the Indians had been beaten and demoralized. It did not occur to him that there was no fight left in the Indians ranged opposite his two regiments, and so he ordered both regiments to leaguer in front of Khem Karan for the night.

At 0200hrs on 9 September, 4th Cavalry and 5th Horse used moonlight and infrared equipment during an attack on the Indian Army's 18th Rajputana Rifles just north of Khem Karan. Indian medium artillery shelled the Pakistani formation, while infantry engaged the enemy armour with recoilless rifles, and the Pakistani tanks failed to

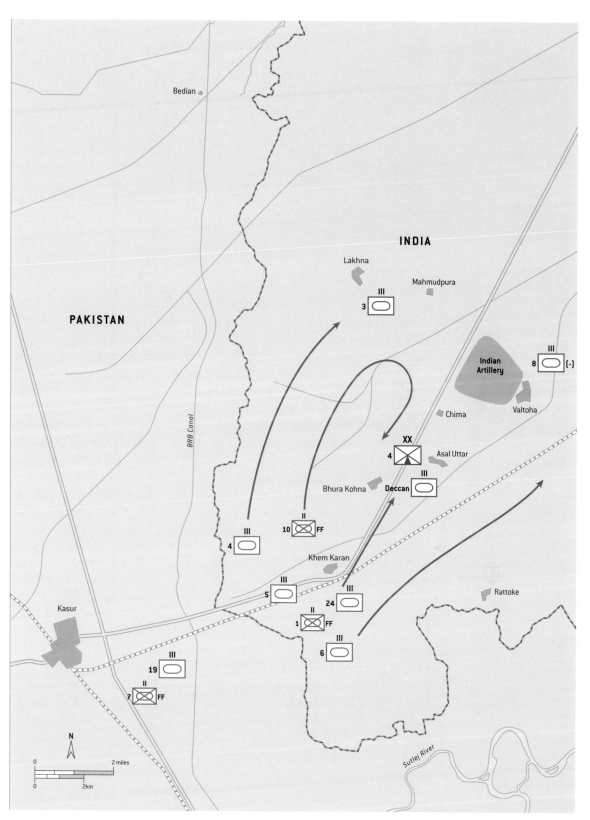

PAKISTAN

INDIA

Bedian

Lakhna

Mahmudpura

3 III

Indian
Artillery

8 III (-)

Chima

Valtoha

XX
4

Asal Uttar

Deccan III

Bhura Kohna

BRB Canal

4 III

10 II FF

Khem Karan

5 III

24 III

Rattoke

1 II FF

6 III

Kasur

19 III

7 II FF

N

0   2 miles
0   2km

Sutlej River

A Pakistan Armoured Corps M47 Patton, marked with a '36' in Urdu in red with white outline. As its auxiliary idler wheel is askew, the track slack and the rear track guard bent upwards, the abandoned vehicle probably struck an anti-tank mine that immobilized it. Essentially an M46 with a T42 turret, the M47 was the last US tank to possess a bow machine gun, as a solid glacis possessed greater structural integrity and strength. Its turret had a lengthy bustle that housed the radio and ventilating blower (with an attached stowage box), a stereoscopic rangefinder within a pair of external blisters, and handles to better accommodate accompanying infantry. The protruding gudgeon near the commander's cupola held a .50-calibre machine gun. While most vehicles used a cylindrical blast deflector, this one has a T-shaped variant, with a bore evacuator just behind. The M47 had offered excellent handling, manoeuvrability, and turret control, but suffered from having a shot trap under its gun shield and poorly arranged ammunition stowage that made it difficult to supply the main gun during combat. (Cody Images)

dislodge the Indian defenders. By 0330hrs Pakistani infantry advanced in APCs, but during their probing they encountered a minefield and withdrew. At 0430hrs, India's 2nd Independent Armoured Brigade was placed under Major-General Gurbaksh Singh's 4th Mountain Division. Orders were issued noting that the Indian armour would operate at night, and that The Deccan Horse would remain in forward defended localities and gun areas in an anti-tank role.

During the night of 8/9 September, Indian Army engineers placed numerous mines to reinforce what were already well-defended positions near Khem Karan. Pakistan's 5th Armoured Brigade undertook the same task as on the previous day, while 4th Armoured Brigade prepared to attack from the left, with the task of severing the Khem Karan–Bhikhiwind road. The M47s of 6th Lancers encountered less opposition than on the previous day and were again able to advance up to Valtoha railway station, while 24th Cavalry to the left (north) was halted at Chima. For the second day in succession, Brigadier Bashir recalled both his armoured regiments back to Khem Karan for leaguer at dusk.

On 9 September a new commander for the Indian Army's 15th Infantry Division, Major-General Mohinder Singh, arrived from Army HQ and tried to boost morale and organize his command. During the afternoon of 9 September, leading elements of 4th Mountain Division mistakenly stopped at a small *nallach* (waterway), short of its canal objective. Following a heavy Pakistani artillery bombardment, Pakistani Pattons suddenly emerged from underneath the canal via ducts the Indian forces were unaware of. The emergence of the tanks unnerved 13th Dogra and this infantry battalion duly abandoned its position. Realizing that desertion was taking a toll on his 4th Mountain Division, Major-General Gurbaksh Singh ordered Brigadier D.S. Sindhu's 7th Mountain Brigade to fall back to Asal Uttar, a village located in the fork of the Khem Karan–Patti and Khem Karan–Bhikhiwind roads and blocking both approaches amid flat, cultivated terrain. Indian Army brigade and regimental officers managed to arrest the problem, often resorting to shaming and calls to honour. With four of 4th Mountain Division's battalions having largely dissolved, XI Corps' commander ordered all but the functional units to be broken up.

THE BATTLE OF ASAL UTTAR

With the Pakistani effort to seize Khem Karan showing promise, the subsequent penetration of Indian resistance along the border would facilitate securing one of the two Beas River bridges some 30km to the east. If successful, the paucity of Indian forces east of the waterway – and the lack of Indian reserves – meant the Pakistani effort could isolate no fewer than 11 enemy divisions – more than half of India's effective strength in the region – and be in a position to move on New Delhi, a mere day's drive away. To prevent such an advance, the Indian Army dug trenches and gun emplacements amid the area's cotton and sugar-cane fields. The area north of Khem

Karan comprised well-irrigated plains crossed by several canals and dykes. Positioned to cover key roadways and approaches, four Centurions of B Squadron, 3rd Cavalry and Shermans of A and B squadrons, The Deccan Horse were deployed in a horseshoe-shaped formation with the opening facing the expected Pakistani advance. Some squadrons were broken up into troops and allotted to 4th Mountain Division, which formed the first line of defence at Asal Uttar. Equipped with jeep-mounted 106mm recoilless rifles, bazookas and other close-range anti-tank weapons, the formation's subordinate units prepared to resist the Pakistani effort, with support from artillery and tank squadrons in the Indian rear.

At 0645hrs on 10 September the final Pakistani attack commenced, with tanks concentrated in the Manwan area, intent on bypassing the Indian-defended sector. Having failed to push through Indian defences directly, Pakistani forces – including 24th Cavalry, 6th Lancers and 1st Frontier Force – moved to outflank 4th Mountain Division. At 0830hrs, a 4th Armoured Brigade battlegroup attacked 4th Grenadiers, but Indian artillery halted the effort before Pakistani infantry could reach the minefield. Indian armour then struck at 24th Cavalry's left flank, which resulted in a tank battle.

The M47 Pattons of Pakistan's 4th Cavalry attempted an outflanking manoeuvre towards Mahmudpura–Dibbipura, which was spotted; India's 3rd Cavalry shadowed the Pakistani movement, and the enemy tanks were finally trapped near Mahmudpura. At 1430hrs Major-General Nasir Ahmad, who had previously watched the battle from a helicopter, came with his reconnaissance group to the Khem Karan–Bhikhiwind road to direct the battle from the ground. 4th Cavalry put in a left hook and reached the objective at 1700hrs, but in the meantime, contact with 4th Armoured Brigade headquarters and 10th Frontier Force, the supporting infantry battalion, had been lost. 4th Cavalry had lost a large number of tanks on the way, owing to the soft nature of the ground, which hindered movement and made them more easily targeted. The tall sugar-cane crop afforded excellent cover to Indian Army recoilless-rifle teams and other small parties who had been unable to withdraw or had decided to fight to the last. 4th Cavalry succeeded in reaching their objective, but had now run out of petrol and were very low on ammunition. Contact with the rear having been lost, no one in the Pakistani regiment knew 4th Cavalry's exact location and no replenishment of fuel or ammunition could be considered. Supported by heavy artillery fire, an Indian infantry battalion, 4th Grenadiers, suddenly attacked Nasir Ahmad's 'R' group, and destroyed it by 1800hrs, killing the general and destroying two additional Pakistani battlegroups; 1st Armoured Division's offensive foundered. According to Indian sources, 75 Pakistani tanks were destroyed or abandoned for the loss of one Centurion and four Shermans.

Having received a serious rebuff on 10 September, 4th Cavalry personnel began surrendering on the 11th. Having striven to capture all territory west of the Beas River and cut XI Corps' rear, six Pakistani armoured regiments – 4th Cavalry, 5th Horse, 6th Lancers, 12th Cavalry, 19th Lancers and 24th Cavalry – had been checked. Instead, the Pakistanis withdrew to Kasur, having lost 97 tanks, including 72 Pattons. This contrasted with the losses suffered during the engagement by India's 4th Mountain Division and 2nd Independent Armoured Brigade, which lost ten and two tanks respectively.

OVERLEAF In support of 4th Mountain Division's stand against attacking Pakistani M47 and M48 tanks near Asal Uttar on 9 September, Centurion Mk 7s operated from hull-down positions amid the area's sugarcane fields, often erecting camouflage netting immediately behind their turrets. Oncoming Pakistani tank crews who were further handicapped by insufficient training on the Patton's rangefinding and targeting controls were hard-pressed to discern targets and formulate a response. Indian 106mm recoilless rifles, soft terrain and an Indian technique of firing three tank rounds in rapid succession to gain a hit first soon eliminated the Patton's purported battlefield invincibility. As is generally the case in such engagements, tank-crew effectiveness was a deciding factor in promoting an Indian victory.

THE SIALKOT FRONT: PHILLORA

OPERATION *NEPAL* BEGINS

Major-General Rajinder 'Sparrow' Singh MVC, GOC Indian 1st Armoured Division, is pictured with a captured M48 Patton from Pakistan's 1st Armoured Division following the battle of Asal Uttar; an Indian Centurion Mk 7 with Type B barrel is in the background. On 8 September, knowing that Pakistan was pushing additional tanks into the battle zone, Rajinder Singh ordered his reserve regiment, 4th Horse, to attack the Pakistani armour from one of the flanks, and placed the unit under command of Brigadier K.K. Singh, commander of 1st Armoured Brigade. At that time, 17th Horse was pulled back to counter a Pakistani threat to Pindi Bhago; 16th Light Cavalry also disengaged and deployed along Hasri Nala. Lieutenant-General Harbakhsh Singh, GOC-in-C Western Command, severely criticized the operation's handling in attempting to rush through Pakistani defences, believing that K.K. Singh had erred in pulling 17th Horse from Tharoh for countering an allegedly serious threat to the left flank at a time when 4th Horse was available, having been released to 1st Armoured Brigade. (bharat-rakshak.com)

At 2300hrs on 7 September the code word 'Nepal' was given, and the Indian offensive was set in motion. By 0300hrs on 8 September, Indian forces had cleared the area from Maharajke to the heavily fortified area around Charwa, having largely overcome elaborate Pakistani defence works, tunnels and stubborn defenders. Having assembled for operations near Ramgarh, at 0600hrs the Indian Army's 1st Armoured Division crossed the international border.

During the night of 7/8 September, Pakistan's 25th Cavalry (attached to Brigadier Abdul Ali Khan's 24th Infantry Brigade) had uncovered 16th Light Cavalry's Operation Order No. 1 from a captured tank, which detailed the Indians' local plan for the day. Just after 0800hrs on 8 September, 25th Cavalry was ordered to counter-attack alone, and did so along a wide front with its three squadrons in line abreast. At 0930hrs, 16th Light Cavalry's leading tanks encountered Pakistani armour, recoilless rifles and entrenched infantry near Gadgor. India later claimed to have destroyed eight Pakistani tanks and two recoilless rifles during the subsequent action. Nearby, 17th Horse encountered similar resistance near Tharoh, south-east of Phillora, and knocked out three Pakistani tanks and a recoilless rifle.

Although the Indian attack had only just penetrated the border, Pakistan reacted sharply to the threat against Sialkot. Within the Sialkot sector, Pakistan had assembled a sizeable force, which included 6th Armoured Division alongside infantry and artillery forces. Massive Pakistani artillery fire was subsequently brought to bear against the Indian incursion in the Sialkot area, but the attackers held what gains they had taken. With the Indian effort having achieved tactical surprise and a bridgehead across the border, 1st Armoured Division now sought to exploit recent successes. Asked to detach some armour, 1st Armoured Brigade sent a contingent to the Kangre area. With much expected of Rajinder Singh's division, sending its lead brigades on divergent, unsupported paths degraded the formation's performance. By dusk on 8 September the Indian tank thrust had stalled, with Pakistan's C Squadron, 25th Cavalry having pushed to south of Chobara before settling into the defensive. During the day, India had lost 12 tanks to Pakistan's 20. As it was, the Indian armoured brigade managed to advance only 7km beyond the bridgehead. Both India and Pakistan had by now played their hand by committing their armoured divisions in the Sialkot and Lahore sectors. Although Indian intelligence had confirmed that Pakistan's 6th Armoured Division was operating in the Sialkot sector, India's own 1st Armoured Division needed to reorganize and replenish before confronting it.

With Pakistani infantry having counter-attacked at Chobara to block the Indians' direct route to Phillora, on 9 and 10 September India's 1st Armoured Division conducted extensive reconnaissance and uncovered an opening in an area near Rurki Khurd, from which to bypass the resistance to the north. A plan was formulated whereby 1st Armoured Division would launch its attack through this unexpected opening to achieve surprise, with 1st Armoured Brigade conducting a demonstration to entice Pakistani armour towards Sabzpir to give the impression of an attack from that direction.

Although the Indian forces were numerically superior to those of their adversary, Pakistani positions blocked a frontage between Lahore and Kasur. Further north at

Sialkot, Pakistani positions were well fortified with wire obstacles, numerous minefields and bunkers, while villages were converted into strongholds complete with underground shelters and interconnected tunnels. Of the Pakistani 6th Armoured Division's three tank regiments, 11th Cavalry at Pasrur was the closest-available unit to relieve 25th Cavalry; all rotations were conducted during the night of 10/11 September.

THE BATTLE OF PHILLORA

At dawn on 11 September, India's 1st Armoured Division launched its attack on Phillora, having achieved surprise, as Pakistani commanders anticipated a thrust from Zafarwal–Phillora or Chobara–Phillora, and had established defences there. By 0500hrs, all Pakistani tank squadrons were in their hastily occupied positions in the area, the terrain flat and featureless, save for crops ready for harvesting. No barbed wire or mines were available to the Pakistanis. Indian forces soon made contact with The Guides Cavalry's Reconnaissance Troop south of Pagowal, which distinguished itself by knocking out two Indian tanks.

Tasked with blocking a Pakistani breakthrough from Gadgor–Lalapur, cutting the Phillora–Chobara road and assisting 43rd Lorried Infantry Brigade, 4th Horse was the first Indian unit to engage Pakistani armour. Having captured Rurki Kalan,

To avoid unnecessary use of a tank's tracks and suspension, or for the purposes of vehicle recovery, a prime mover with trailer was commonly used for tank transportation. Here, a Centurion Mk 7 works with what appears to be a Thornycroft Antar 60-ton tractor, with a Dyson eight-wheel trailer. Note the circular aerial identification friend or foe marker, makeshift muzzle cover and single counterweight on the fume extractor. The Tank No. 15 Mk 1 periscope is to the right of the identification marker, while the sighting scope is just forward of the cupola. (Simon Dunstan)

Looking east from near Phillora. Early on 11 September, India's 4th Horse and 17th Horse conducted a pincer movement against Pakistan's 11th Cavalry and 9th Frontier Force as they defended the area, having replaced 25th Cavalry and 24th Infantry Brigade the night before. Nearby, 16th Light Cavalry was ordered to prevent Pakistani armour from interfering with the main operation. (Umar Bajwa)

C Squadron, 4th Horse pushed for Wachoke, just north of Phillora, as A and B squadrons, 4th Horse headed towards Saboke from the north-east; 4th Horse's regimental headquarters advanced between A and B squadrons from the east of Rurki Kalan. A squadron of Pakistani armour awaited the attack between Libbe and Kotli Khadim just to the east. One tank with 4th Horse's regimental headquarters knocked out three Pakistani tanks, while A Squadron advanced to within a kilometre of the road and engaged Pakistani armour there. C Squadron was asked to join B Squadron's right. During the tank battle, 29 Pakistani tanks were claimed as destroyed; 4th Horse lost three tanks. Meanwhile, 17th Horse had moved on to the Libbe axis to join the Indian assault, taking up position on 4th Horse's right. 16th Light Cavalry established a roadblock near Khananwali, while 62nd Cavalry moved to the Pagowal crossroad to protect 1st Armoured Division's western flank.

At 0700hrs, Pakistan's 11th Cavalry reported knocking out two Indian tanks. At 0817hrs, C Squadron, 11th Cavalry encountered Indian forces between Phillora and Libbe; three Pakistani tanks were destroyed and two tanks damaged, and in a subsequent skirmish the squadron lost three more due to recoilless-rifle and tank fire coming from Libbe. Soon after, a strong Indian force moved on Phillora; at 0830hrs, as the Indian armour approached, the Pakistani infantry company at Josun buckled and withdrew with few casualties. At 0900hrs, a heavy Indian artillery barrage masked Indian tanks moving up to Phillora. With several officers of 11th Cavalry killed or wounded, Pakistani command and control in the area was severely disrupted. The artillery fire took a heavy toll on C Squadron, 11th Cavalry deployed along the Bedian–Phillora railway tracks, with nine of its 11 M36B2 tank destroyers and seven M48s knocked out, at no cost to the Indians.

At 0900hrs, 17th Horse's forward elements encountered Pakistani armour along the Libbe–Kotli Bagga line. As the attack commenced, intense Pakistani artillery fire staggered the assault line and inflicted heavy casualties. The Indian brigade commander, Brigadier K.K. Singh, thus tried to clear Khananwali and Wachoke first to facilitate a smooth advance. One troop from C Squadron, 17th Horse was to support an attack put in by two companies of 5/9th Gorkha Rifles. Two troops of Pakistani Pattons attacked from the right, but C Squadron, 17th Horse countered their effort. Having established itself at a crossroads to cover 1st Armoured Brigade's right, 62nd Cavalry (minus C Squadron) commenced its attack at 0930hrs along the Kaloi–Haral–Pagowal crossroads and secured Haral; although the unit was later forced from its crossroads position, it accomplished its goal of protecting 1st Armoured Brigade's flank.

OPPOSITE With Pakistan's Operation *Grand Slam* having stalled before Akhnur, India transitioned to the offensive just to the south against Pakistani forces in the Sialkot area. On 7 September, 1st Armoured Division, with 14th Infantry and 6th Mountain divisions in support, struck across the international border. Compelled to reposition two armoured regiments from the Akhnur sector to stem the Indian advance which approached Chawinda on 10 September, Pakistani formations were forced back on Phillora where armoured and infantry reinforcements effected a firm defence that would hold until the cessation of hostilities on 23 September.

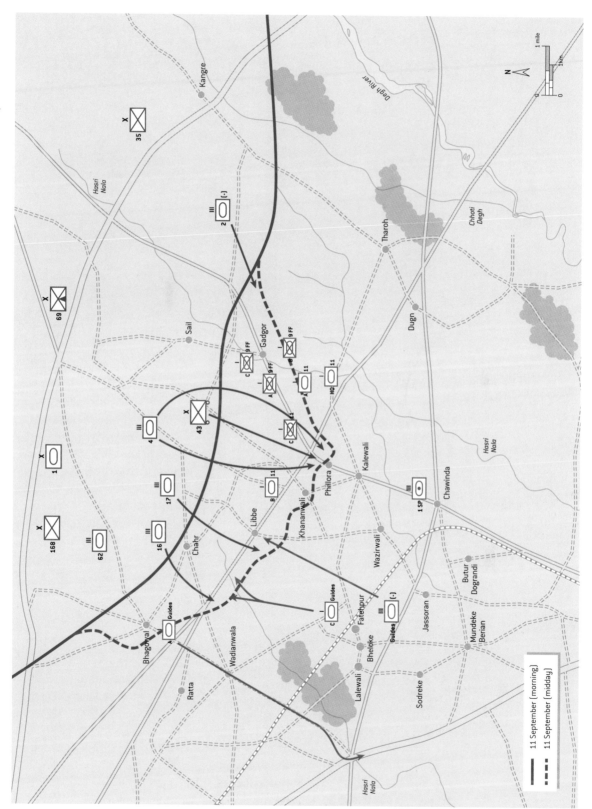

11 September (morning)

11 September (midday)

65

The strong Pakistani brigade group at Zafarwal would secure the Pakistanis' eastern flank, while repositioning 24th Infantry Brigade and 25th Cavalry to Pasrur was intended to provide depth and a mobile strike force. Pakistani forces in the area were short of infantry to develop much-needed pivots at Bedian and Chawinda, however, and one battalion/regiment group at Phillora appeared too weak a force for the extended positions it was required to occupy. These weaknesses were somewhat compensated for by the strong divisional force of The Guides Cavalry and 22nd Cavalry (M48 Patton), and one mechanized-infantry battalion, 14th Frontier Force. With the Pakistani defence in the balance and its Reconnaissance Troop already in action – knocking out three Centurions – The Guides Cavalry had been alerted to be prepared to conduct a counter-attack with infantry support. This Pakistani effort to counter the Indian thrusts largely succeeded in stalling the Indians in their effort to push further south. By 1130hrs, however, 11th Cavalry had become disorganized; the regiment was ordered to collect its remnants and rendezvous south of Chawinda. 25th Cavalry was ordered to the Phillora–Chawinda area to provide armour for that fight. The Pakistani defence between Chawinda and eastern Sialkot was thin and covered by 25th Cavalry and 11th Cavalry but no infantry. 14th Frontier Force was rushed to Chawinda, as was 24th Infantry Brigade, with 14th (Para) Brigade ordered from Zafarwal to Pasrur.

At 1135hrs, 25th Cavalry set off for Chahr and Libbe; M48s of A Squadron reached Chahr, while after crossing the railway line, Major Ziauddin Ahmad Abbasi's B Squadron ran into Indian anti-tank fire, suffering several casualties as a result, including its commander. A strong Indian armoured column moved from Bejragarhi to Pagowal. 25th Cavalry claimed 21 Indian tanks destroyed for the loss of just six of their own; the Pakistani regiment's actions helped stabilize the Pakistani defence, but it could not prevent Indian forces from infiltrating to the Phillora crossroads.

In light of the developing situation, B Squadron, 17th Horse was ordered to move up and deploy to the west of C Squadron to deal with Pakistani forces there.

Pictured at Phillora, this Pakistani M48 Patton was destroyed by an APDS round from a Centurion of 4th Horse. The regiment, some of whose members are pictured here, later used the photo on their December 1965 Christmas card, with the caption: 'When the Cents went Marching In'. The photo's contributor is at the far right. (Major Karun Khanna (Retd))

Following 5/9th Gorkha Rifles' effort to clear Libbe and the surrounding sugar-cane fields, accomplished by 1230hrs, C Squadron, 17th Horse advanced on Phillora, while B Squadron held an anchoring position at Libbe. When C Squadron had pushed east of Libbe, Pakistani tanks engaged it from 800m; in retaliation, the Indian squadron destroyed three Pakistani tanks and captured one. Nine Pakistani tanks arrived to counter the Indian regiment's progress. C Squadron then claimed to have destroyed seven of the enemy tanks. Information was received that one squadron of Pakistani tanks was moving from Alhar towards Phillora, and B Squadron adjusted to meet the threat; A Squadron moved up two tank troops to guard B Squadron's western flank, just as two Pakistani tank troops emerged from Kot Izzat, seemingly intent on taking C Squadron in the flank.

Open terrain and sugar-cane fields separated the combatants, and helped mask movement until a sudden engagement at just 100m erupted, lasting for 45 minutes until the surviving tanks withdrew. Lieutenant-Colonel A.B. Tarapore, CO 17th Horse, knocked out two Pakistani tanks early on; all told, 28 Pakistani tanks were destroyed against only one from 17th Horse. The Pakistani armoured thrust was defeated, and the defensive crust around Phillora was breached. The objective was now open to an Indian infantry assault.

At 1400hrs, 11th Cavalry received orders to move. Pakistani ground reconnaissance had not been conducted during the day, however, and several delays and miscommunications between 9th Frontier Force and 11th Cavalry meant the unit didn't move for several hours. Major-General Abrar Hussain, GOC 6th Armoured Division, was not informed of these issues. At 1530hrs, 43rd Lorried Infantry Brigade secured the Phillora crossroads for India. Pakistani armour had been badly mauled, with as many as 67 tanks destroyed or damaged during the day for the loss of six Indian Centurions. In coordination with 4th Horse and 17th Horse, which were responsible for 1st Armoured Brigade's left and centre, 16th Light Cavalry was to

CENTURION FIRING PROCEDURE

During targeting, the gunner needed to account for a variety of ballistic factors, including barrel droop, air density, wind, target range and movement (if any), and gun wear that progressively reduced muzzle velocity by some 30.5m/sec after firing 150 APDS rounds. The Centurion also lacked a trunnion tilt corrector for use when firing from a position other than level with the horizon.

The Centurion's electric turret traverse was backed by a manual cranking wheel. Getting rounds on to the target quickly equated to survival on the battlefield; instead of having the M47 and M48's more sophisticated optical rangefinders, Indian gunners had no direct sight, and relied on a Mk 1 or Mk 1/1 periscope to visually determine the target's range, followed by three 20-pdr rounds in quick succession. Thoroughly practised, this 'blind technique' typically resulted in the enemy tank being struck first, meaning that – providing the azimuth was correct – a 'kill' could be achieved at ranges in excess of 2,000m. During such actions, the loader deposited spent shell cases through the pistol port and reorganized the sliding bins, as the ventilators struggled to clear the vehicle of cordite fumes.

cover the right, in particular the road junction near Khananwali, to prevent Pakistani armour from breaking through from Sialkot. A squadron of Pakistani tanks as well as recoilless rifles attacked B Squadron, 16th Light Cavalry; Pakistani losses were six tanks and three recoilless rifles, while the Indians lost four tanks.

On reaching Phillora at 1700hrs, 25th Cavalry was moved to the village's east to extricate 9th Frontier Force; the Pakistani battalion was encircled and wireless contact was intermittent. By late afternoon Pakistani information was sketchy and confused; 11th Cavalry milled about towards Pasrur when the regiment was supposed to be near Chawinda, and was in no condition to fight on. As darkness fell at about 1900hrs on 11 September, a general silence descended, with 13 M48s having been knocked out during the day (seven from 11th Cavalry and six from The Guides Cavalry) along with nine M36B2 tank destroyers from 11th Cavalry; this represented more than one-third of 6th Armoured Division's total casualties

M48 FIRING PROCEDURE

The M48's fire-control system components were added in four phases, starting with a T35 sight – later the M20 (×6 and ×1 magnification). As a pendulous periscope it presented some difficulty in adjusting the line of sight in elevation, but was superior ergonomically compared to straight telescopes, as the eyepieces moved forward and back rather than up and down during vertical changes in the main gun. This reduced gunner fatigue, and avoided the need for a glacis or mantlet aperture that would degrade armour integrity. Phases II and III replaced the commander's T161 sighting and target-designation telescope with what had been the M47 gunner's stereoscopic T46E1 direct rangefinder. The targeting system's override facility allowed the commander to turn the turret towards a threat, after which the gunner would fine-tune and engage. A T24E1

ballistic drive was also incorporated and connected the gun-elevation mechanism with the M20 sight and T25 range drive. A final phase substituted the T30 ballistic computer for the T25. A T156E1 telescope was also used for direct sighting, while indirect fire-control components included a T28 azimuth indicator, an M13 elevation quadrant and an M1 or M1A1 gunner's quadrant for calculating trajectories.

On selecting a target, the commander announced the type of ammunition to be used, which the gunner then indexed into the T30 ballistic computer, while the loader added the round into the breech. The T46E1 rangefinder mechanically transmitted target distance to the T30 ballistic computer from which elevation information went to the T24E1 ballistic drive which adjusted the main gun to position the reticle.

during the war. Conversely, the Pakistanis estimated Indian losses to be in the region of 30 to 45 tanks. Owing to tank losses suffered by The Guides Cavalry and 11th Cavalry, and breakdowns involving all but five of its M36B2 tank destroyers, 11th Cavalry was to be temporarily broken up, with a squadron of M48s transferred to The Guides Cavalry. The tank destroyers were formed into a group and sent to support Pakistani artillery around Pasrur. Although Indian forces had failed to exploit their success around Phillora, excellent Indian gunnery, skilful tank manoeuvring and inspired junior leadership contributed to their victory, and seemed to promise future gains.

THE SIALKOT FRONT: CHAWINDA

THE FIGHT FOR ZAFARWAL

A series of tank skirmishes now occurred west and south of Phillora, as Indian armour regrouped for a renewed attack. The Pakistani regrouping on 11 September had left Zafarwal essentially undefended. At 0630hrs on 12 September, Indian artillery targeted Zafarwal, but by 0800hrs the Indian attack was repulsed. During a lull in the fighting, 3rd Armoured Brigade (19th Lancers, 7th Frontier Force and 16th (SP) Field Regiment) moved into 6th Armoured Division's area and was subordinated to the formation, but the Pakistani brigade was not to be committed to battle without approval from I Corps HQ.

At 0900hrs there was a second Indian assault at Zafarwal from the same direction, but with more tanks; although this was rebuffed, it was followed two hours later by a forceful Indian armoured assault from the direction of Bhindial, involving two Sherman squadrons of 2nd Lancers, closely followed by an infantry battalion and supported by artillery. In response, 4th Frontier Force, supported by 22nd Cavalry's M48s and 33rd TDU's Shermans, knocked out a dozen Indian tanks and captured three, with no Pakistani tank losses. At 1500hrs, Pakistani aircraft reported a concentration of about 30 to 50 Indian tanks and 1,000 infantry near Track Junction headed for Zafarwal, which Pakistani commanders believed was 1st Armoured Division's diversion, as the main Indian formation was making for the Chawinda–Bedian region. At 1700hrs, 1st Armoured Division began its creeping advance along the Kalewali–Sainewali road south-west of Phillora, and by last light fell back to its firm base for the night.

Following Zafarwal's capture by Indian forces, Pakistan's 14th (Para) Brigade recaptured the settlement with little difficulty by 0100hrs on 13 September, while to the west 1st Armoured Division manoeuvred as a pincer, using 43rd Lorried Infantry Brigade from the north and 99th Mountain Brigade and 1st Armoured Brigade from the north-west, to strike for Chawinda. 1st Armoured Division was to cross the Sialkot–Chawinda–Pasrur railway line to encircle the town from the west as a preliminary move prior to launching the main Indian attack. By 1600hrs, 69th Mountain Brigade had been bombarded by roughly 1,000 artillery shells around Koga and Mile 54, when Pattons of B and C squadrons, 22nd Cavalry with infantry support counter-attacked from the south-west, advancing about 1,500m from the forward defended localities before being halted by Indian artillery and armour.

Considering the cupola machine gun has been removed, and given the exposed nature of the Indian soldier from The Dogra Regiment and the camera person, this appears to be a staged photo of an abandoned Pakistani M48. The soldier's hand is on one of the vehicle's three turret lifting eyes; two more lifting eyes on the mantlet were used to remove the barrel. Note the absence of turret markings and the canvas mantlet cover. (bharat-rakshak.com)

THE FIRST BATTLE OF CHAWINDA

The Indian offensive began at dawn on 14 September; soon after, Indian armour encountered a Pakistani anti-tank screen north of Alhar and west of Phillora. During the morning of 14 September, the Indians probed Chawinda from the west, but The Guides Cavalry and 25th Cavalry held them in fighting that lasted until midday. After an early-afternoon lull, at 1530hrs the Indian offensive resumed, starting from Wazirwali–Kalewali and aimed between Chawinda and Fatehpur, where 24th Infantry Brigade waited. This would involve overrunning Jassoran and outflanking Chawinda from the west. Pakistan's 25th Cavalry, 32nd TDU and 3rd Frontier Force (from the east) and The Guides Cavalry and a squadron from 11th Cavalry (from the west) halted the Indian thrust in a series of fierce tank engagements; during the evening the Indians withdrew to Phillora–Kalewali. An additional Indian thrust from near Pagowal to cut the Sialkot–Bedian road formed the attackers' outer prong. By dusk, 1st Armoured Division had secured Kalewali and Alhar after claiming 18 Pakistani tanks destroyed, as well as several recoilless rifles and equipment. The battle's progress fell short of Indian expectations, as Indian armour failed to create the tactical preconditions for an infantry assault on Chawinda. 43rd Lorried Infantry Brigade's attack was subsequently called off.

An Indian crew operating their US-provided 106mm M40 recoilless rifle during the fighting around Chawinda. Such weapons were often mounted on vehicles, such as this M38A1 Jeep. (bharat-rakshak.com)

Having requested additional tanks, on 15 September Indian forces made fresh attempts to capture Chawinda, putting in an infantry/armour attack from Wazirwali and Kalewali, with 25th Cavalry and Pakistani infantry putting up a spirited defence. At 0800hrs a second Indian attempt tried to drive a wedge between Jassoran and Chawinda, but this too was repulsed. Pakistani infantry and a troop from 25th Cavalry countered an Indian feint north-west of Chawinda. With Indian attacks against Chawinda being blunted, they began redirecting their efforts towards Bedian. The Guides Cavalry was now reduced to two weak squadrons covering a wide area from Jheje to Jassoran. Fighting continued until around 2100hrs.

THE SECOND BATTLE OF CHAWINDA

On 16 September, Indian forces launched three major coordinated attacks on Bedian and Chawinda: the first between 0730 and 1030hrs, a second from 1230 to 1430hrs, and a final one from 1630hrs until dusk. The Indians used a weak regiment to attack 22nd Cavalry Group at Bedian, and attempted to break through The Guides Cavalry in the centre. With the Indian right flank covered near Bedian, A Squadron, 17th Horse and C Squadron, 4th Horse then thrust southwards for Butardograndi before taking a now isolated Chawinda. Pakistan's defences held, and reinforcements were brought up later. A large Indian tank column made some gains along the axes Fatehpur–Sodreke–Mundeke Berian and Janewal–Jassoran–Butur Dograndi, but suffered losses in the process.

The Indian anti-clockwise movement to envelop Chawinda was led by 4th Horse on the outer circle, with 17th Horse on the inner one. The Indians continued to advance against what seemed to be weakening Pakistani resistance and resolve, as evidenced in part by elements of 3rd Frontier Force breaking and fleeing their trenches between Chawinda and Butardograndi. With so few Pakistani infantry west of Chawinda, Indian forces captured Jassoran at 1000hrs. A follow-up Indian attack on Butur Dograndi resulted in another tank battle. 19th Lancers could not halt the Indian thrust, and during the confusion the Pakistani regiment was mistakenly engaged by tanks of 25th Cavalry. Butur Dograndi duly fell to the Indians. Between 1230 and 1400hrs there was continued fighting around Bedian, but the Pakistani defence largely held. At 1630hrs, with the Pakistani position faltering, Brigadier Abdul Ali Malik, commander of 24th Infantry Brigade, expressed doubts about being able to hold his position and unsuccessfully sought permission to withdraw from Chawinda. Pakistani artillery fired at Indian armour at Butur Dograndi from some 1,500m, which halted the Indian movement. 25th Cavalry tanks engaged as well, and this artillery/tank combination knocked out four Indian tanks; 24th Cavalry then stemmed the advance in this sector.

Lieutenant-General Dunn, GOC I Corps, met with 1st Armoured Division and 6th Mountain Division at Maharajke to discuss fresh plans for Indian forces to capture Chawinda, Bedian and Zafarwal. 6th Mountain Division was tasked with taking Chawinda, while 1st Armoured Division and 14th Infantry Division moved on Bedian and Zafarwal, respectively. Since 6th Mountain Division's 69th and 99th Mountain brigades were already committed elsewhere, 35th and 58th Infantry brigades were reallocated to Major-General Korla's 6th Mountain Division from 1st Armoured Division. As a preliminary to launching an attack on Chawinda, Indian forces captured certain villages; these would serve as pivots to attack Chawinda, and to counter any Pakistani attempts to interfere. In a series of brisk actions, 1st Armoured Division employed 4th Horse, 17th Horse and 8th Garhwal Rifles, securing the villages by dusk against stiff resistance. Pakistan lost 28 tanks during the day. Several Indian commanders were also killed. During the night of 16/17 September, 1st Armoured Division headquarters misunderstood the reallocation of 35th Infantry Brigade to 6th Mountain Division, and moved the brigade forward from Gadgor to Phillora as part of a preliminary attack move before the brigade returned to its original location, thereby wasting valuable time.

After three days of heavy fighting, 17 September was relatively calm, with only minor repositioning. The Pakistanis had halted the Indian assault on Chawinda, but it had created a large penetration between Bedian and Chawinda. Localized Pakistani counter-attacks achieved little, and Indian armour and infantry held all their gains against tenacious Pakistani attacks. Tank battles raged throughout the morning and afternoon, with both sides losing eight vehicles each. 6th Mountain Division was to effect its attack on Chawinda while 1st Armoured Division held key villages west of Chawinda to cover Korla's command until it captured the settlement. However the attack, slated for the night of 17/18 September, was again postponed for 24 hours. After Major-General Rajinder Singh stressed that his 1st Armoured Division had been holding villages west of Chawinda and would be hard pressed to continue doing so, the division was withdrawn from two of the villages; but it retained Jassoran at all costs, as this represented a firm base of operations for the Indian infantry.

According to 1st Armoured Brigade, conditions during 14–17 September had been favourable for an infantry assault on Chawinda, as it and Bedian had been isolated and cut off from three sides, following 1st Armoured Brigade's having invested both from the rear, particularly on 16 and 17 September. Roughly two Pakistani infantry companies held the area near each objective, but as these were reinforced, applying Indian armour was considered unwise, and an opportunity was lost. Even so, although Pakistan forces had halted the Indian offensive in the Sialkot region, they had shot their bolt and were exhausted. Pakistani armour had been battered, and stocks of artillery ammunition were nearly expended.

STATISTICS AND ANALYSIS

COMMAND FAILINGS

During the relatively brief, limited-scope conflict of 1965 the forces of both sides exhibited bravery and perseverance; but inconsistent, often self-defeating behaviour was evident among the senior leadership, with many commanders lacking modern combat experience,

Major R. Christian and Brigadier Hari Singh (at left) of the Indian Army examine a Pakistani M47 (vehicle number 30) which had been knocked out during the fighting around Phillora. Note the tank's cylindrical blast deflector and the British-supplied Sten submachine gun with a 32-round magazine over Singh's shoulder. With an effective range of just 100m, the Sten would be used for close defence.
(bharat-rakshak.com)

and possessing an inadequate appreciation of the role of air power in supporting ground operations. Much of this resulted from border skirmishing and security duties having failed to provide sufficient conventional battlefield experience to junior and senior officers, and the lack of the logistics, resource allocation and other factors necessary to achieve combat success. The 1965 fighting emphasized defence over the more complicated offence, due primarily to the British colonial military/security experience, the similarity of weapon systems, and the pre-1947 experience of fighting division- and brigade-level defensive battles until overwhelming superiority permitted tentative offensive action. While intelligence gathered by both sides was frequently processed and analysed slowly, both armies' principal reason for failure was a seeming inability to act decisively: to exploit, integrate and leverage tactical success and turn it into operational victory.

For India's forces, division- and brigade-level intelligence and a lack of command resolve hindered their ability to aggressively pursue a breakthrough in the Gadgor area when they had the means and opportunity to do so. Similarly, at Asal Uttar, such cautiousness and poor staff work resulted in a Pakistani failure to concentrate all five of its armoured regiments on 8 and 9 September to achieve a tactical breakthrough, and thus avoid entrapment and defeat; this was duly exploited by the Indian higher headquarters at division, corps and army level. President Ayub Khan decided to replace Major-General Malik with Major-General Yahya Khan as Operation *Grand Slam*'s commander at a time when Pakistani forces were poised to capture Akhnur during the middle of the fighting on 2 September, and Yahya Khan subsequently called a temporary halt to organize and resupply his forces; these actions enabled the Indian defenders to trade space for time in which to allocate reserves and bolster their positions. Pakistan's unwillingness – or inability – to quickly secure the key transportation hub ultimately proved to be a Pakistani staff and planning failure in which all – from brigade level to GHQ – were included, while the Indian failure was a command failure in which the prime culprits were the armoured brigade and divisional commander. At Chawinda the Indian approach was sluggish, cautious and complacent; Lieutenant-General Dunn, GOC I Corps, seemed disinterested in participating in the battle, and communication between GOC 6th Mountain Division and GOC 1st Armoured Division was lacking. Despite the qualitative and numerical superiority of Pakistani armour, the Indians prevailed in the Lahore and Sialkot sectors, while halting Pakistan's counter-offensive on Amritsar; even so, India's tanks were sometimes employed in a faulty manner, such as charging prepared defences during the defeat of Pakistan's 1st Armoured Division at Asal Uttar.

TANKS AND CREWS

Turning to the tanks involved: much like the World War II-era T-34 and Panther, the Centurion possessed an excellent balance of armament, armour protection and manoeuvrability. Initially outfitted with a 17-pdr gun which had proved effective for the early 1940s battlefield, the advent of post-war Soviet vehicles such as the Soviet IS-3 heavy tank necessitated the Centurion's incorporation of a 20-pdr cannon and eventually a NATO-standard 105mm L7. The Centurion was simpler to operate than the M48, and engaging targets required less training to remain competitive in securing a hit first – especially

Captured Pakistani M48 Pattons ('24' and '35') at 'Patton-Nagar'. Note that the vehicles' machine guns have been removed. Although the M48 Patton represented a formidable weapon system in the right circumstances and when manned by a skilled, well-trained crew, in the combat environment in which the 1965 tank clashes occurred, the Centurion proved superior. On viewing the remnants of destroyed and disabled Pakistani armour at Bhikhiwind, the Indian President, Dr Sarvepalli Radhakrishnan, commented, 'Born in Detroit, died in Bhikhiwind.'(bharat-rakshak. com)

with the Centurion Mk 7, which was considered very effective by its crews. In addition to the Centurion, India's use of the AMX-13 light tank, with its 75mm L/70 copy of the main gun used on the German Panther, and iterations of the M4 Sherman proved effective against Pakistani armour when employed in a manner that minimized the Indian tanks' deficiencies.

Initially, Indian forces – especially tank crews – demonstrated a wariness for engaging Pakistan's M48 Patton; this was understandable, considering the US tank's lauded sophistication and combat effectiveness. The M48 Patton was faster and better equipped than the Centurion, had greater manoeuvrability, and featured an infrared periscope enabling night operations. The M48 Patton was well suited for offensive operations within a limited battle zone, and in an effort to accurately target enemy armour at greater distances, as the M41 gun was considered to have a 70 per cent chance of achieving a hit; the tank possessed an advanced fire-control system that included a stereoscopic rangefinder, mechanical ballistic computer, ballistic drive and a gunner periscope. The M48's mechanical ballistic computer took into account ballistic influences imparted by vehicle cant and different ammunition types; and linked to the drive, it automatically elevated the gun. As the 1965 fighting wore on, however, the M48 was found not to be as invincible as had been professed, for in the noise and chaos of fluid combat such systems, despite seeming on paper to be combat assets, frequently proved to be overly burdensome. (The ballistic computer found on the Soviet T-62 would create similar problems for Arab tank crews during the 1967 and 1973 wars against Israel.)

Outnumbered Pakistani Pattons performed very well with 25th Cavalry and the regiments of 6th Armoured Division, as demonstrated by the division knocking out 180 Indian tanks for the loss of 61 of its own between 10 and 23 September, the latter figure comprising 31 M48s, 17 M47s, nine M36B2s and four Shermans; many of the Indian tanks were Centurions Mk 7s of 17th Horse and 4th Horse. Pakistan's squadron-level and small-unit leadership proved superior during the Akhnur battle, in which engagement tactics depended on squadron, troop and individual tank commanders' skills in attack or in defence. One tank in the right place could create considerable carnage, but its success depended on a well-trained and experienced crew. As was common during combat, a numerical or technological advantage could be negated by a motivated, determined force. Ultimately, harnessing the M48's sophistication was not beyond the Pakistani crews that manned them, but rather was hampered by the lack of proper crew training.

AFTERMATH

Although the 1965 war was essentially a draw, India achieved its limited war aims by preserving the status quo in Jammu and Kashmir, and successfully countering Pakistan's attempt to overrun and secure the area. East Pakistan was not attacked, and the Pakistan Navy was held back from offensive action. The Indian Air Force was not employed until 6 September; if it had launched a full-scale pre-emptive attack that day against its Pakistani contemporaries, and if the Indian Army had launched a full-scale offensive after 20 September, Pakistan's battlefield position would have become increasingly untenable – but at a cost to both sides. By late September, the prospect of a lengthy, attritional war increasingly softened the militaristic stance of both sides, and made the third UN resolution attempt in as many weeks palatable. At 0330hrs on 23 September, quiet descended across the front lines; to date India's I Corps had taken some 500 square kilometres of Pakistani territory, and (by Indian estimates) destroyed 144 enemy tanks, along with large quantities of arms and ammunition, at the cost of 29 Indian tanks, with another 41 damaged. On 10 January 1966, the Indian Prime Minister and Pakistani President met in Tashkent, Uzbekistan, at the invitation of the Soviet Chairman of the Council of Ministers, and finally formulated an agreement that both sides would return to their respective positions held on 5 August 1965.

The struggle for Jammu and Kashmir remained an unresolved bone of contention, however, and in 1971 a third war erupted, which like the previous conflict was characterized by poor command and control above regimental level, and an inability or unwillingness among the senior leadership to act decisively during key moments.

As a system for accumulating, evaluating and applying battlefield experiences was lacking, little had changed from World War II-era British-inspired methodologies, or 1965 doctrine, tactics and logistics, and past failures were often repeated with similar results.

Given that offensive actions were generally more complex to undertake effectively than the more stationary defence, Pakistan's opening attack against an Indian outpost at Longewala on 4 December 1971 typified much of the new fighting – but having neglected to conduct sufficient reconnaissance of the terrain and environment over which they would be assaulting, the attackers' unsophisticated midnight frontal assault was soon stymied when 23rd Infantry Division halted before unexpected barbed-wire entanglements, and what were assumed to be integrated minefields along the attack axis, while 65 accompanying tanks struggled to manoeuvre through the soft terrain. Emboldened by the Pakistanis' lack of success, the outnumbered Indian defenders remained in their exposed position to await support if possible. With Pakistani intelligence having failed to anticipate the degree to which Indian air power would support its ground forces, at dawn Indian Air Force aircraft arrived to hinder further the Pakistani attack and buy time for proper Indian reinforcements to arrive. With 23rd Infantry Division's frontal attacks blunted, the formation's commander was inspired to reorganize elements into what was an effective battlegroup, which struck further south in a flanking manoeuvre that paralyzed the Indian commander's ability to react to the threat.

Along the northern section of what had expanded into the Shakargarh Bulge, near the 1965 Sialkot battleground, the battle of Barapind–Jarpal (Basantar) perhaps best illustrated the shortcomings of senior leadership on both sides, and the resulting high casualties sustained for what was gained. Senior Pakistani commanders maintained a belief that armoured formations were better used to smash an enemy force using physical strength rather than thrust through its weak zones to maintain freedom of

Produced in huge numbers, the Soviet T-54/55 main battle tank – shown here on 1 December 1971 – began production in 1947 and was exported to several countries during the Cold War. The vehicle's 100mm D-10T2S cannon and small cast turret made it a relatively small target, with a low silhouette. In contrast to the 1965 Indo-Pakistani War's more tentative, set-piece actions, the 1971 fighting in East Pakistan witnessed fast-paced, predominantly infantry operations, in which Pakistani forces in the west launched an attack in the Shakargarh sector to divert Indian formations from the primary battle zone. In an effort reminiscent of Operation *Grand Slam*, Pakistan once again attempted to secure the fertile Jammu and Kashmir area, and physically block India's main supply route into the mountainous Kashmir region to the north. (AFP/Getty Images)

A Centurion Mk 7 pictured during the fighting in 1971. Note the driver's head protruding from the hull to improve his visibility. While India fielded its Soviet-supplied T-54/55 tanks in 2nd Armoured Brigade, 16th Independent Armoured Brigade relied on older Centurion Mk 7s, which also squared off against their old M48 adversaries in Pakistan's 8th Armoured Brigade. (Simon Dunstan)

manoeuvre and attack softer command and logistical targets; this meant that the Pakistani assault near Chumb would not repeat Operation *Grand Slam*'s successes, scored against defending Indian armour mostly comprised of the lightly armoured AMX-13. For the operation, 8th Infantry Division's cumbersome configuration of four infantry brigades covered the Shakargarh Bulge, with 15th Infantry Division defending the approaches to Sialkot; 8th Armoured Brigade's 13th Lancers, 27th Cavalry and 31st Cavalry, with 15th (SP) Regiment and the infantry of 29th Frontier Force provided a potential counter-attack force. Although I Corps technically included 17th Infantry and 6th Armoured divisions, in practice these formations represented a Pakistan Army strategic reserve that had been positioned in the Pasrur–Daska–Gujranwala area.

To contest the Pakistani incursion, the Indian Army deployed its 36th, 39th and 54th Infantry divisions, along with 2nd and 16th Independent Armoured brigades and assorted artillery and engineer elements. During the subsequent fighting, India's six armoured regiments and two independent reconnaissance squadrons were pitted against Pakistan's five armoured regiments and one independent squadron from 8th Infantry Division, as well as 8th Armoured Brigade and four armoured regiments from 6th Armoured Division. Where Pakistan intended to use I Corps to defend the Shakargarh area as a reaction to anticipated Indian efforts aimed at eliminating the bulge, India attacked along the protrusion's northern and eastern sections to fix the Pakistani defenders and better secure their main supply route into Kashmir.

Indian forces, possessing a numerical advantage in infantry, were soon able to push the Pakistanis from much of the bulge, although minefields, trenchworks and concrete bunkers conspired to hinder further Indian tactical manoeuvre and progress. During an attack, generally conservative brigade and division commanders on both sides were overwhelmed when faced with having to control multiple subordinate formations; this was made evident when I Corps at Shakargarh failed to commit more than one armoured regiment at a time, and when Pakistan's reserve 6th Armoured and 7th Infantry divisions were never even committed to the fight. Eventually, numbers won out and Indian forces achieved success in that sector. Lasting just 13 days, the 1971 conflict was one of history's shortest wars. Whereas the 1965 war had ended in a draw, in 1971 the swift Indian defeat of Pakistani forces in East Pakistan – now an independent Bangladesh – effectively eliminated half of Pakistan's population and a large portion of its already limited economy. With the struggle for Jammu and Kashmir continuing to the present, India and Pakistan, like so many other countries, became saddled with an ongoing war for which no clear success criteria or exit strategy had been formulated.

BIBLIOGRAPHY

Ahmad, Saeed (1971). *Indo-Pak Clash in Rann of Kutch*. Rawalpindi: Army Education Press, GHQ.

Amin, Agha Humayun, Maj (Retd) (2000). 'Grand Slam – A Battle of Lost Opportunities'. *Defence Journal*, Vol. 4, No. 2, September 2000. http://www.defencejournal.com/2000/sept/grand-slam.htm (accessed 8 May 2015).

Amin, Agha Humayun, Maj (Retd) (2013). *The Tank Attack That Failed*. Self-published.

Bajwa, Farooq (2013). *From Kutch to Tashkent: The Indo-Pakistan War of 1965*. London: Hurst & Co.

Brines, Russell (1968). *The Indo-Pakistani Conflict*. London: Pall Mall.

Gupta, Hari Ram (1967). *India–Pakistan War, 1965*. Vols I and II. Delhi: Hariyana Prakashan.

Hu, C.J., Lee, P.Y. & Chen, J.S. (2002). 'Ballistic Performance and Microstructure of Modified Rolled Homogeneous Armor Steel'. *Journal of the Chinese Institute of Engineers*, Vol. 25, No. 1: 99–107.

Hunnicutt, R.P. (1984). *Patton: A History of the American Main Battle Tank*. New York, NY: Presidio.

Husain, Abrar (2006). *Men of Steel: 6 Armoured Division in the 1965 War*. Oxford: Oxford University Press.

Khan, Mohammed Asghar, Air Marshal (Retd) (1979). *The First Round: Indo-Pakistan War 1965*. Noida: Vikas.

Laible, R.C., et al. (1980). *Ballistic Materials and Penetration Mechanics*. New York, NY: Elsevier Scientific.

Munroe, Bill (2005). *The Centurion Tank*. Ramsbury: Crowood Press.

Musa, H.J. Muhammad (1985). *Jawan to General: Recollections of a Pakistan Soldier*. Srinagar: ABC Publishing House.

Pradhan, R.D. & Chavan, Y.B. (2007). *1965 War, the Inside Story: Defence Minister Y.B. Chavan's Diary of India-Pakistan War*. New Delhi: Atlantic Publishers & Distributors.

Sandhu, Gurcharan Singh, PVSM, Major-General (Retd) (1987). *The Indian Armour: History of the Indian Armoured Corps, 1941–1971*. Vols 1 and 2. Delhi: Vision Books.

Singh, Bhupinder. Colonel (Retd) (1982). *1965 War: Role of Tanks in the India–Pakistan War 1965*. Patiala: BC Publishers.

Singh, Harbakhsh, Lt Gen (Retd) (2012). *War Despatches: Indo-Pak Conflict 1965*. Delhi: Lancer.

Suttie, William (2015). *The Tank Factory: British Military Vehicle Development and the Chobham Establishment*. Stroud: The History Press.

Zukas, Jonas A., ed. (1990). *High Velocity Impact Dynamics*. New York, NY: Wiley-Interscience.

MILITARY PUBLICATIONS

Chakravorty, B.C. (1992). *Official 1965 War History*. Ministry of Defence, Government of India, History Division.

Chief of Army Field Forces (US) (1951). Report of the U.S. Army Policy Conference on Armor. Copy #93. Fort Monroe, VA.

US Army Research Office (1954). Report, Tank vs Tank Combat in Korea.

US Army Research Office (1961). Ogorkiewicz, Richard M. *Armored Vehicles and Armor*.

US War Department Equipment Board (1960). Development of 90mm Gun Cannon, T208 Series, TIR 1-1-2H1(3).

War Office (UK) (1943). 232/36. Tank Policy, Director of the Royal Armoured Corps.

War Office (UK) (1948). Code 1881. User Handbook for the Centurion I, II and III.

War Office (UK) (1953). Code 10538. User Handbook for Tank, Med. Gun, Centurion, Mk 3, 5 and 6.

War Office (UK) (1954). 194/516. Tests to investigate necessity of modifications to Centurion tanks to accept type B 20-pdr gun barrel fitted with fume extractor.

War Office (UK) (1955a). 194/340. Offensive firing trials against Centurion 3 tanks.

War Office (UK) (1955b). Regulations for Army Ordnance Services. Volume 4 – Ammunition. Pamphlet 8. Q.F. Fixed Ammunition. Part 9 – Cartridge, Q.F., 20-Pr.

War Office (UK) (1958a). Code 11653. User Handbook for the Centurion Mk 7 and 8.

War Office (UK) (1958b). 185/305. Supply and Manufacture of Centurion tanks for India 1954 May–1958 Jan. 406/Policy/218.

INDEX

References to illustrations are shown in **bold**.